What Happened After Letting God
The road traveled by A Course in Miracles student.

Author: Nick Arandes

© copyrighted 2019

For information visit: www.NickArandes.com

Order this book online at www.nickarandes.com Most titles are also available at major online book retailers.
© Copyright 2019 Nick Arandes.

If you purchased this book without a cover you should be aware that this book may have been stolen property and reported as "unsold and destroyed" to the publisher. In such case neither the author nor the publisher has received any payment for this "stripped book."

This book contains copyrighted material. All rights reserved. No part of this book may be reproduced in any mechanical, photographic, or electronic process, or in the form of a phonographic recording nor may it be stored in a retrieval system, transmitted, or otherwise be copied for public or private use other than for a "fair use" as brief quotations embodied in articles and reviews-without prior written permission of the publisher and/or author. Violators of copyright law will be prosecuted.

Note for Librarians: A cataloguing record for this book is available from Library and Archives USA Printed in USA
ISBN-9781798100271

We believe that it is the responsibility of us all, as both individuals and corporations, to make choices that are environmentally and socially sound. You, in turn, are supporting this responsible conduct each time you purchase one of our books, or make use of our publishing services.

Our mission is to efficiently provide the world's finest, most comprehensive book publishing service, enabling every author to experience success. To find out how to publish your book, your way, and have it available worldwide, visit us online at www.kdp.amazon.com

The intention of the author is only to offer information of a general nature to help you in your quest for a deeper understanding. What is outlined in this book is practiced by the author on a daily basis. In the event you use any of the information contained in this book, the author and the publisher assume no responsibility for your actions. The author wants also to make clear that the principles outlined here, although based on the teachings of A Course in Miracles, does not make the author an authority on The Course. He is simply sharing his own understanding of what The Course teaches as well as his experiences as a result of practicing and applying the principles contained in The Course.

To order additional products or services visit: www.NickArandes.com

Book cover designed, illustrations and formatting by the author.

Table of Contents

Acknowledgments ii
Preface 1
Introduction 3
What Happened After Letting God 5
Who I Am or What I Am 11
Duality and Non-Duality 17
Mind, Ego and the Holy Spirit 21
Unconscious Guilt 29
The Avoidance of Pain and The Pursuit of Pleasure 35
True Forgiveness 39
Common and Not So Common Questions 47
1 How did A Course in Miracles originate? 48
2 Why is the Course so difficult to understand? 48
3 Who is the Son of God? 52
4 What is sin? 54
5 What is the miracle? 54
6 Example of everyday life to illustrate how true forgiveness would be implemented. 56
7 Why is it that I do not experience results when putting true forgiveness into practice? 59
8 What then is the purpose of forgiveness if it will not change anything in my dream? 60
9 How was it that the mind decided to dream this dream of separation? . 60
10 Is there anything wrong with asking for something you want? 61
11 Where do desires come from? 63
12 I feel a great passion for what I do, do I still have to practice forgiveness? 64
13 If a person or situation causes me pain and I practice forgiveness, am I supposed to feel something after doing the process? 65
14 I feel like I'm struggling with my financial situation and I do not understand how remaining in peace can help me. 66
15 How can I differentiate between the ego and the Holy Spirit when I make a decision? 67
16 If I feel a strong attraction towards someone, is that my ego? 68
17 What does it mean to change the purpose of a relationship? 68
18 How is a special relationship different from a holy relationship? 70
19 What happens if my partner is not spiritual like me: should I stay with her or him? 71

20 How can I deal with people who bother me, who press my buttons, who do not respect my space, etc.? 72
21 How can I discipline my children and do it peacefully when in reality what I feel is frustration and anger when they behave in a certain way? 73
22 How is it possible that at times I could manifest things easily and now I feel I cannot manifest anything? 74
23 While I practice forgiveness and I let go, how can I manage my life? . 75
24 If everything goes well in my life, I love what I do, I enjoy the money I make, I love things as they are, is there anything wrong with experiencing that life? 75
25 Is there male and female energy? 76
26 I have been taught that prayer is an integral part of my spiritual development, but if everything is an illusion, what would be the purpose of prayer? 77
27 I have a partner that I love. I also have friends that I love. Then there are people that I do not know, as well as people that I do not like. How then is it possible to love everyone in the same way? 77
28 I would like to be in a relationship. Should I go out into the world and do something so that this experience can take place? 79
29 Should I or should I not study with another teacher or attend another seminar? 79
30 What does it mean that there is no order of difficulty in miracles? 80
31 How do I know I'm ready for this awakening process? 81
32 How can I prepare myself for the awakening process? 81
33 How long will it take to wake up from this dream? 81
34 When I see war and conflict in the world, how do I respond to it? 81
35 How is it possible that some people say they see a beautiful world while what I see is destruction? 82
36 How do I know if I am advancing on my spiritual path? 83
37 I'm confused about the difference between creation and projection. If I'm projecting something, is it not the same as saying that I'm creating it? .. 83
38 What does cause and effect mean according to A Course in Miracles? 84
39 I consider myself a healer and I have been practicing for many years. Now I am confused because if everything is an illusion, does that mean that I should stop doing the work I love so much? 86
40 If the body is an illusion, does that mean that I can eat what I want? And what about being a vegetarian or being aware of the foods I eat to keep my body healthy? 87
41 How does the Course address reincarnation and, consequently, karma? 88
42 What could be said about why babies are born with severe defects? ... 88

43 It is said that God projected this world to be able to experience its opposite and thus have the experience it could not have in a state of unity. How does A Course in Miracles address this statement? 89
44 How does A Course in Miracles address the issue of abundance, especially when it is said that service to others is the key to experiencing it? 89
45 Are there people through whom God communicates? 90
46 If I love the ego can I heal it? 91
47 If meditation is a means of contacting my Self, is there any specific way to practice it? And if so, how much time should I devote to meditation, how regularly should I do it, and what kind of responses should I expect to receive? 91
48 I feel confused about the subject of sex. It feels so good. However, is it another distraction from awakening? 92
49 I have been told that I must be aware of my actions because they can affect other people. 93
50 I wonder if this information could be explained to a child of three to ten years. To all the children that I know this information would be very confusing. How could I go about it? 94
51 How is it possible that I can perceive oneness, unity, when my eyes are seeing separation? That being the case, how is it possible to practice unity? What did Jesus see when he was interacting with other people? 94
52 How can I move around the world without judging? 96
53 If everything I see is a reflection of me (as part of the same mind), does this mean that the way others act or feel is a representation of what is in me? 97
54 If I am reacting while someone is yelling at me how can I perceive love, knowing that love is the only thing that is real? 98
55 What to do when one is trapped in "the dark night of the soul"? 99
56 How to approach the death of a loved one? 101
57 I do not understand what is meant by a divided mind since God is all that exists. 102
58 Now that I have become a dedicated student of A Course in Miracles, I feel that I do not belong anywhere, as if I have nothing in common with others. Can you offer any suggestions on how to deal with that? 104
59 What would A Course in Miracles say about homosexuality? 105
60 I have heard that when one goes to sleep and begins to dream, that is the space in which the soul plays because it has been released from the body. Is it like that? 106
61 How do I know if it is the voice of the ego or the Holy Spirit that I am listening to? 106
62 Is there what might be called a "healthy" or "benevolent" ego? 107

63 I've heard a lot about gratitude; that if I want my life to change I have to be grateful. And yet, no matter how grateful I try to be, most of the time my life does not seem to improve. 107
64 How does the Course in Miracles see the idea of positive thinking? . 107
65 What is it to be a teacher of God? A teacher of God is the individual who demonstrates the pri.. 108
66 What does the Course mean when it says "infinite patience produces immediate effects (T-5.VI.12: 1)"? 109
67 How to receive the guidance of the Holy Spirit? 109
68 If the ego is a belief, and all beliefs can be changed, can I not then change the belief that I am, or that I have an ego with the belief that I am one with God and, therefore, eradicate the ego completely? 110
69 When babies are born, are they born innocent?.....................................111
70 If I put the Course into practice, can I heal my body? 112
71 Does intuition exist? 113
72 What does the Course mean when it says: Do not fight against yourself?
....114
73 What does A Course in Miracles mean when it says that the curriculum is highly individualized? 115
74 What is love? 116
Conclusion 119

A Course in Miracles' second edition consist of the *Preface*, part I also known as the *Text*, part II: the *Workbook for Students*, part III: The *Manual for Teachers*, and finally the *Clarification of Terms*.

The third edition of the Course has two additional addendums, which consist of *The Song of Prayer* and *Psychotherapy: Purpose, Process and Practice*. There is an earlier version, which is referred to as the Original Edition.

The abbreviations below apply to the second and third edition because some the original information were omitted from the first draft due to the fact that were mostly messages for Bill and Helen, which, if included in the final draft would have confused students of the Course.

The following symbols are used to find in a course in miracles any excerpts cited in this book:

T: Text (Part I of the Course)
W: Workbook for Students (Part II of the Course)
M: Manual for Teachers (Part III of the Course)
C: Clarification of Terms
S: *Song of Prayer* (An addendum to A Course in Miracles)
P: *Psychotherapy: Purpose, Process and Practice*

Example: T-29.V.5:4-8 means: Text, Chapter 29, Section V, Paragraph 5 Sentences 4 to 8.

W-pI.100.2:3 means: Workbook for Students, Part I, Lesson 100, Paragraph 2, Sentence 3.

M-4.2:3 means: Manual for Teachers, Chapter 4, Paragraph 2, Sentence 3.

T-25.In.3:1-2 means: Text, Chapter 25, Introduction, Paragraph 3, Sentences 1 and 2.

C-in.4:1-5 means: Clarification of Terms, Introduction, Paragraph 4, Sentences 1 to 5.

Acknowledgments

Before beginning any acknowledgment, I would like to bring something to your attention. Although I am not a scholar in the English language I feel I am fluent enough to express myself in such a way that would be acceptable and comprehensible to anyone who feels the inspiration to read any of my books. I love to keep a sense of closeness and casualness with my readers, just as I feel when I am giving a live talk.

It was challenging for me to find an editor who could respect my style of writing without wanting to change it into something that when I read it I felt it was not me. Fortunately, life presented me with an angel by the name of Leigh, who, aside from having a proper command of the English language, understanding my dilemma, she took upon herself the task of focusing strictly on grammar, while keeping my style of writing style intact, only offering suggestions when she felt that a particular idea may not have been clearly expressed. Therefore, I want to acknowledge and thank from the bottom of my heart **Leigh Longhurst** for her kindness and willingness to proofread this book.

Being aware that we are all part of the same Essence, I thank all those who, in some way, have had any contact with me, brief or extensive, direct or indirect, as all these people have played a significant role in my process of healing. This gratitude also includes *you*, reader, for allowing me to share the content of this book, reminding you that I am *not* your "teacher", but that together we walk hand-in-hand with the *One* Who holds in "us" the memory of *True Love*.

Preface

If you read my previous book "*What Happens When You Let God*", you will be aware that what I share is based on the teachings of *A Course in Miracles*. I have never considered myself a spiritual teacher or facilitator of the Course. I consider myself rather someone who practices it, whose desire is to experience the love that, according to all kinds of spiritual philosophies, is our true nature.

However, inexplicably, I have found myself playing the role of someone who is sharing the teachings of the Course. And instead of struggling with or resisting this role, I have been trusting that by sharing its theory, in private or publicly, whilst putting the principles into practice, it is the perfect curriculum through which I can integrate what the Course is teaching.

For people who are not familiar with *A Course in Miracles*, I would like to emphasize that the Course is just one of many paths, not "the only path". That's why the Course states: "*Although Christian in statement, the Course deals with universal spiritual themes. It emphasizes it is but one version of the universal curriculum. There are many others, this one differing from them only in form. They all lead to God in the end*". (Preface ACIM). This being the case, I will use the Course's teachings as a reference.

My desire with this book is to close the circle that began with my earlier publication. If for any reason some of the content in my previous book led to a misinterpretation of the purely non-dual teaching of the Course, here it will be rectified.

If I am inspired to write more books, I have a feeling that I will stop using the Course's terminology for two reasons: firstly *A Course in Miracles*, to my understanding, has only *one* Teacher, the Holy Spirit in Course terminology; and secondly, I do not want people to consider me a "teacher" or "facilitator" of the Course. Such a stance might keep the student distracted by focusing on me instead of the message that the Course, impeccably dictated, attempts to convey. However if I am supposed to share the teachings of *A Course in Miracles*, that will take place, not because it is my intention, but because it will be orchestrated by love itself for the benefit of remembering ***Who, or What I really Am.***

Introduction

During my years of spiritual searching, beginning in the late 1980s, I entered the world of contemporary metaphysics and spirituality, following different paths in search of peace, abundance, happiness, love, or whatever else I thought I was looking for. Only after completely surrendering did A course in Miracles appear in my life.

Although all these philosophies and practices that I studied and participated in served as steps to help me look at life in a different way, I could not deny the fact that I did not feel fulfilled. I felt something was missing; I was not happy and I was not at peace. I had to put aside all that I had "learned" in order to open myself to the understanding that I will share in this book. A Course in Miracles says: *"Yet the essential thing is learning that you do not know. Knowledge is power, and all power is of God. You who have tried to keep power for yourself have "lost" it. You still have the power, but you have interposed so much between it and your awareness of it that you cannot use it. Everything you have taught yourself has made your power more and more obscure to you".* T-14.XI.1: 1-5.

The power to which this extract from the Course refers is not something that you "have". It is what you are! I identified myself so much with the content of the Course, that as I was putting it into practice, I felt inspired to write *"What Happens When You Let God"*. The original English version consisted of three parts. The first and second parts focused on explaining the theory of the Course, according to my understanding at that time, as well as how I applied it to different aspects of my life. The third part addressed questions I had, not only about the teachings of *A Course in Miracles* for those who felt inclined to study the Course, but also related to the field of metaphysics and the world of self-help in general. When I started to translate the book into Spanish, I felt it was better to put all those questions and answers aside so that at some point in the future, when I honestly felt the impulse, I would do a review and then publish them.

All these questions are now added to the content of this book, answered from a clearer theoretical understanding, as well as from experiences lived as a result of putting the Course's teaching into practice, always emphasizing that the Only Authorized Source, according to my understanding, to teach *A Course in Miracles* is the Holy Spirit. That is why we are reminded, *"To change your mind means to place it at the disposal of true Authority"*. T-1.V.5: 7

If you resonate with the content in this book, and therefore feel the inspiration to read and study *A Course in Miracles*, I would humbly suggest that you give it the time and dedication necessary so that you can get the benefit of the Course's teaching. With the wish that love and peace reign forever in you, I would like to begin by briefly sharing ***what happened after letting God***.

What Happened After Letting God

When I read *A Course in Miracles* and began to put it into practice, I was aware that nothing that happened in the world had the power to make me happy or to give me peace; only a change of mind could do it. However, I needed to have experiences so that this understanding could be integrated. As circumstances in my life began to change (not because I read and practiced *A Course in Miracles* since I am aware that the Course has nothing to do with what happens in the world of form, which will be explained later) I realized why the changes were taking place. It felt like I was being given the opportunity, in my own lived experience, to see that only an internal shift could offer me the peace and happiness I was so desperately seeking. As I mentioned at the beginning, although theoretically I was already aware of it, I still needed the direct experience.

Before my circumstances began to change, my experience was not comfortable because life for me had stopped making sense. I had no desire to do anything. There was even a moment when I was caught by a feeling of darkness, and the only thing I could do was surrender completely to the experience. Therefore, when I felt that my life was not "working", when things were going "wrong", I felt lost. However when things started to change for the "better" I realized that even then I was not at peace and still unhappy. That led me to pose the question "What is it that I truly desire"?

Thanks to the experiences that were taking place, I became fully aware that unless I made inner peace the most important thing for me, I was going to spend the rest of my life oscillating between what I thought I wanted and what I thought I did not want. From 2007, when *A Course in Miracles* came into my life and I wrote my first book, until December 2010, not only was I jobless, except when something sporadically appeared allowing me to earn enough to cover my basic needs, I didn't even have enough money to pay rent so I stayed with friends or acquaintances. I had to declare bankruptcy for the second time. According to how things looked, I felt that unless something miraculous happened, there was no possible way for me to get out of my situation.

In 2010 I was presented with the opportunity to visit Spain and give some talks. As a result, I felt inspired to translate my book *"What Happens When You Let God"* into Spanish and to share my theoretical comprehension of the teachings of *A Course in Miracles* to the Spanish-speaking community through social media like Facebook and my blog. This was all done without any intention, or personal agenda. I was simply doing what I felt inspired to do. Questions began to emerge from people who resonated with what I wrote. I would share my comments with no intention of seeking followers or promoting myself.

In January of 2011 I was invited to give a talk in Mexico City. From that day until this, by invitation only, I have given talks in the United States, Mexico, Guatemala, Panama, Costa Rica, Venezuela, Colombia, Argentina, Uruguay, Chile, Peru, Canada, Spain, England, Germany, Holland and other countries whose invitation I declined, mainly because I feel more and more inclined to bask in the silence. That does not mean that I will stop giving talks. I may stop or I may not; that is beyond my control. As you read the contents of this book you will understand why.

I have generated enough money to have a savings account and be able to enjoy a life that is at least more "normal". Thousands of people throughout the world follow my writings and appreciate everything I share; moreover, they open their hearts to me and share their concerns. I have had the opportunity to have relationships, established new friendships and am constantly invited to do television, press and radio interviews. Everything I pursued in the past has become my present life experience, and yet all these experiences, however "exciting" they may appear to be, could, if I am not conscious, serve as a distraction from what is really important, inner peace.

As my internal process deepened, I could clearly observe that the world, with all its distractions, has nothing of value to offer, nothing I really desire, as we are reminded in lesson 128 of *A Course in Miracles*: *"The world you see holds nothing that you need to offer you; nothing that you can use in any way, nor anything at all that serves to give you joy. Believe this thought, and you are saved from years of misery, from countless disappointments, and from hopes that turn to bitter ashes of despair. No one but must accept this thought as true, if he would leave the world behind and soar beyond its petty scope and little ways"*. W-pI.128.1: 1-3. Obviously, you cannot stay there because you would end up depressed; as cited in lesson 129: *"... This is the thought that follows from the one we practiced yesterday. You cannot stop with the idea the world is worthless, for unless you see that there is something else to hope for, you will only be depressed. Our emphasis is not on giving up the world, but on exchanging it for what is far more satisfying, filled with joy, and capable of offering you peace. Think you this world can offer that to you?"* W-pI.129.1: 1-4.

So when things in my life went "wrong", it was easy to desire inner peace and put into practice the teachings of *A Course in Miracles*. However, my desire for the world and its pleasures was still latent, just buried in the unconscious. Once the doors began to open up for me, and all these new experiences started to manifest, I became aware that peace and happiness could not be derived from anything the world could offer. This comprehension settled in as a result of direct experience, not as theory. It served as a motivation to fully delve into the path I am now sharing in this book.

This takes me back to a conversation I had with an old friend when I was living in Florida. Although at the time of the conversation I recognized that I was not equipped to understand his dilemma, now it makes perfect sense. We were sitting on the doorstep of his house and he said to me: "There must be something else, because I have reached all my goals, I have all the money I longed for and still, I feel there is something missing." In *A Course in Miracles*, Jesus, Holy Spirit, Inner Wisdom is not in opposition to our desires, although he knows very well that they lead nowhere. Until we become ready to listen to him, he patiently awaits our readiness to follow his teachings. He says: *"If you want to be like me I will help you, knowing that we are alike. If you want to be different, I will wait until you change your mind. I can teach you, but only you can choose to listen to my teaching"*. T-8. IV.6: 3-5.

I cannot deny that there were many moments when I experienced confusion, since on the one hand there were things that I apparently still wanted while simultaneously, I knew that they had nothing to offer and therefore I had no will to chase them. Inner peace was becoming a priority for me while at the same time I still wanted experiences the world had to offer. *A Course in Miracles* addresses this state of confusion by stating: *"As this recognition becomes more firmly established, it becomes a turning point. This ultimately reawakens spiritual vision, simultaneously weakening the investment in physical sight. The alternating investment in the two levels of perception is usually experienced as conflict, which can become very acute"*. T-2.III.3: 7-9.

I still have the experiences that every person has; desires arise because as long as I continue to experience myself as a "human being" desires are part of that experience. Actually, it is not the body that experiences desires; they are generated in the mind and are experienced through the body. That is why *A Course in Miracles* is mind training, not physical training. The difference is that as I (the mind) become more consciously aware, there is recognition of the power within me to choose how to live each experience. When any desire arises, it can be observed innocently, allowed to continue its course without having to act upon it. I am not talking about ignoring desires or suppressing them. What I am saying is, now they can be observed, and as a result they no longer have the power that was previously attributed to them. Those same desires can now serve as pointers to Truth when placed under the right guidance.

Without a change of mind, you may not be able to understand

what I just shared, so maybe it won't make any sense to you right now. As a matter of fact, in some people it could generate fear. But I can assure you that it is the most liberating experience. Once you have the direct experience of living this way, you cannot conceive of living otherwise. So do not be surprised if, as a result of this new awareness, you find yourself wondering: *"How could it possibly be that I lived a whole life thinking the way I used to?"*

So, what happened after letting God? Well, generally I experience more inner peace. That's it. There were no "angels" sounding trumpets to show me the way, I did not become "enlightened" (according to most people's definition of enlightenment), I saw no flashes of light around me, I did not magically attract money and problems did not disappear. I have simply learned to be at peace with what is. As the mind continues to heal, unconscious fears have continued to arise, only now they are seen as obstacles that emerge to be released.

I recognize that we all want to find some "magic wand" that frees us from fear. But what we fail to recognize is that we invented fear. The Course reminds us: *"It has already been said that you believe you cannot control fear because you yourself made it, and your belief in it seems to render it out of your control. Yet any attempt to resolve the error through attempting the mastery of fear is useless"*. T-2.VII.4: 1-2.

Therefore, we must choose a New Teacher with Whom to look at the content of our mind, a subject I will explore later. If something I have shared so far has aroused some sense of discomfort, just remember that if you are happy and at peace, there is no need for you to continue reading this book unless you feel inspired to do so. But if you are not experiencing peace, the words contained in this book may serve as a flash of light that could illuminate the path. Not because "I", the character Nick Arandes has written them, but because together we walk holding the Hand of the One Who accompanies us, and Who in turn, will use symbols such as books, words, images, or whatever else facilitates our becoming conscious of our True Essence.

Before continuing with the next chapter, I would dare to say that the change of mind that I have been experiencing has not taken place as a result of reading books, attending workshops, or following "spiritual teachers", although I recognize that everything has been an integral part in the process. Rather it has been as a result of making peace my utmost priority. That´s why *A Course in Miracles* says: *"Knowledge is not the motivation for learning this course. Peace is"*. T-8.I.1: 1-2. While the world's distractions may prove irresistible to the "individual character" you mistakenly take yourself to be, they are easily transcended by the You (uppercase) that you truly are. And that True Identity of which I speak has nothing to do with this physical experience. So, let's explore together then, this concept of **Who I Am or What I Am.**

Who I Am or What I Am

Given that *A Course in Miracles* is a purely non-dual teaching, it is important to understand to what or to whom the Course's message is directed. It is certainly not to the "I" who thinks he is writing these words, nor to the "you" who thinks he is reading them. Let's explore briefly then, the idea of Who I Am or What I Am.

That which You (uppercase) are, although it has been called by many names, is nothing more and nothing less than God (Love). Why is it impossible for us to experience our True Essence at our present level of experience? Well, imagine the light itself asking the question "Where is the light?" or "What is the light?" The mere fact that the light is asking this question means it is not allowing itself to be experienced as light, since the question itself is the denial of its true identity.

That is why *A course in Miracles* is not interested in answering the question "What or Who am I?" but rather it focuses on removing the interference so that the experience of what I Am can be revealed. The Course states: "*The course does not aim at teaching the meaning of love, for that is beyond what can be taught. It does aim, however, at removing the blocks to the awareness of love's presence, which is your natural inheritance*". T-In.1: 6-7.

Therefore we will explore the possibility of being aware, at least at the intellectual level, of what we really are in a way that reflects in our attitude. But again, for the record, at this physical level we cannot experience our reality for reasons that will be clarified later. The analogy of the dream, in my opinion, is the simplest and best way to explain the inexplicable. However it is not one hundred percent representative of non-duality, because when one speaks of someone dreaming a dream, there is the one who dreams the dream and the dream itself. This is by definition a dualistic statement. Nevertheless I will refer to this analogy when addressing some of the questions presented in this book.

In the next chapter I will discuss further what is meant by dual and not dual. For now, let's start laying a foundation that will not affect the message that I intend to convey in this book.

Imagine you say to me, *"Last night I dreamed that I was at a party talking with some friends."* If you are not aware, you will not be able to recognize that in this sentence you are talking about two "me's" that are diametrically opposed. To be more precise, one of them is real and the other does not even exist! All fear derives from the fact that this 'detail' is completely overlooked. Let's then divide the sentence so that it begins to make sense to you. Using the following drawing as a reference, first you say, *"Last night I dreamed ..."* Who are we referring to? We are referring to the one who is in bed sleeping, the only one dreaming, as seen in the following illustration:

Then you say that *"I was at a party talking to some friends."* At that moment you forget that you are the one who is dreaming the dream and identify yourself with an image within the dream.

Who I Am or What I Am

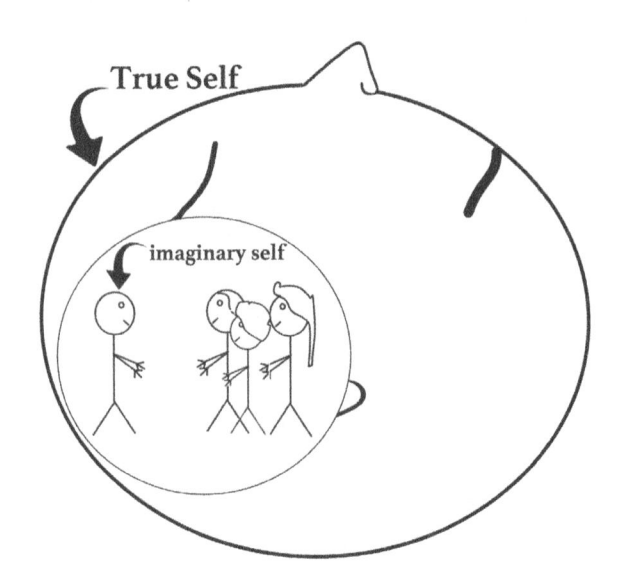

That's why *A Course in Miracles* states: "*Nothing real can be threatened. Nothing unreal exists. Herein lies the peace of God*". T.In.2: 2-4

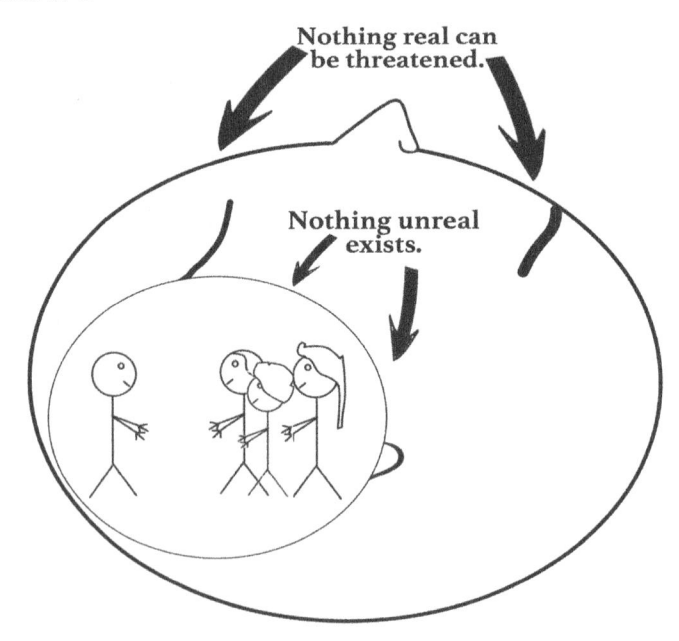

To bring this understanding to the level at which we appear to be, the "you" that appears to be reading this book as well as the "me" that appears to have written it, are being imagined by the only mind that is dreaming this dream. That is what makes "you" and "me" part of the same Source. That is why it is said that we are all One.

As long as I believe myself to be the character that writes these words in the same way that you believe yourself to be the character that reads them, the mind that dreams this dream is distracted. This means that nothing I do in this world helps me to awaken to my reality, because what I believe I'm doing here requires the mind to put all its focus on this dreamed "I".

It is very important to be aware of the fact that what wakes up from the dream is neither the "you" who thinks it is reading these words nor the "me" who thinks it wrote them. What has to awaken is the mind that is dreaming "both". Otherwise we will try to apply the message of the Course to the world of effects, to the character that is being dreamed instead of to the mind that is the cause of the projected dream. That's why *A course in Miracles* says: "*This is a course in cause and not effect*". T-21.VII.7: 8.

As mentioned earlier, it is necessary to be aware of who or what the Course is speaking to. That is the fundamental error, the typical confusion in levels to which one can easily succumb when one takes the Course personally. That is what attempting to bring Truth to illusions consists of. The Course puts it this way: "*When you try to bring truth to illusions, you are trying to make illusions real, and keep them by justifying your belief in them. But to give illusions to truth is to enable truth to teach that the illusions are unreal, and thus enable you to escape from them. Reserve not one idea aside from truth, or you establish orders of reality that must imprison you. There is no order in reality, because everything there is true*". T-17.I.5: 4-7.

I highly recommend that you give yourself a moment of silence to reflect on what you have just read. I feel it would be best if you reread this chapter a couple of times before continuing.

Now it is time to clarify something of enormous importance. When we speak of Truth (uppercase), of God (Love) and of non-duality, there is no "dreamer" dreaming anything. God, Truth, Love, simply Is, and having no beginning or ending, it is unlimited. This is another characteristic of that which is non-dual: it has no limits; it has no borders; it is all that there is; it is eternal. The character that I drew dreaming the dream, even when the dream has not been projected in his mind, is dual because it represents a separation. "Separation from what?" you may ask. The answer is separation from the space that contains it, since the "dreamer" has to be inside some "place" so that he can be labeled "dreamer". Therefore one could deduce that there is the apparent separation wherein there seems to be a part of the Whole (dreamer), separate from the Whole dreaming a dream, as we can see in the following illustration:

> That within **All That There Is**, although I gave it the shape of a face, is only an idea within **All That There Is**. That is what dreams the dream. That would be the first sign of an apparent separation, but in truth, the separation never occurred.

Dream within "All That There Is" which dreams the dream

As demonstrated in this illustration, the separation we are talking about never took place. That is why when we talk about this physical experience we talk about it being an illusion, a dream. This is not because it is perceived as a dream or because it is perceived as an illusion but because it does not exist!

A Course in Miracles puts it this way: *"The ego will demand many answers that this course does not give. It does not recognize as questions the mere form of a question to which an answer is impossible. The ego may ask, "How did the impossible occur?", "To what did the impossible happen?", and may ask this in many forms. Yet there is no answer; only an experience. Seek only this, and do not let theology delay you*". C-In.4: 1-5.

What this extract means is that if one engages in debate about the nature of our "existence", the mind will keep running in circles, getting nowhere. Rather, let us put all our focus on the recognition of Truth and not allow the theology (concepts, beliefs and opinions) to delay us from that process. In my talks, I always explain that what interests me is not knowing what will take place after leaving this physical experience, but rather experiencing the peace and happiness to which I have access now, and at all times. Otherwise, we will forever be preoccupied by new theories on the subject, and the peace and happiness of which I speak will forever elude us. It can only be experienced as a result of letting everything (concepts, believes, opinions, rationalization) go. In other words, the highest form of teaching is silence.

I feel that this is not the time to go further into the meaning of letting everything go. I just want you to have a good foundation so that, as you continue reading, all the pieces of the puzzle will fall into place. Trust the process. Let's now elaborate briefly on the difference between what is known as *duality and non-duality.*

Duality and Non-Duality

Non-dual means that there is only one. Yet this would not be an inaccurate way to describe non-duality, because it is not even that there is one, since the concept 'one' is still a quantifiable object. That is why when we talk about God (what is non-dual) it is said that God Is. Not that God is this or that. It simply Is and there is nothing else! If you experience any resistance when using the word God to describe non-duality, you can replace it with the word Love. If so, the word Love should be written in uppercase so as not to be confused with a feeling or a human sentiment, as it would conventionally be described.

A Course in Miracles does not try to speak about or describe non-duality (Truth, Love, God) because that is impossible. It reiterates this multiple times, beginning with the introduction to the textbook when it says: "The course does not aim at teaching the meaning of love, for that is beyond what can be taught. It does aim, however, at removing the blocks to the awareness of love's presence, which is your natural inheritance". T.In.1: 6. Another example is to be found in this excerpt from chapter 18 where it says: "*This course will lead to knowledge* (to what God [Love] Is), *but knowledge itself is still beyond the scope of our curriculum. Nor is there any need for us to try to speak of what must forever lie beyond words*". T-18.IX.11: 1-2. Notwithstanding that language - being part of this dual experience - limits us, we are going to use it to at least point in the direction of what is known as non-duality.

To return to the analogy of the dream, when you sleep and dream, how many are dreaming the dream? The answer is obvious: one. There are no opposites, only one mind, that of the dreamer. However, within the dream it appears that there are "many" objects, persons, events etc. But it is still only one mind dreaming the dream. Duality is governed by perception. For perception to take place there must be two, the subject (the one who perceives) and the object (that which is perceived). In this physical experience, the self that I believe myself to be, although it is an object since it is a dreamed figure, an image, just like the rest of the 'world' is known as 'the subject' and whatever I believe I am perceiving is known as 'the object'. I, with my eyes, perceive a car that is in front of me. "I" am the subject, the "car" is the perceived object. I, with my ears, listen to the neighbors laughing. "I" am the subject and the "sound", the laughter of the neighbors, is the perceived object. I feel the warmth or the coldness of the water when I put my hand in it. "I" am the subject and the "feeling", the warmth or the coldness of the water, is the objective quality of the sensation.

Then there is the perception of opposites - high-low, ugly-beautiful, fat-skinny, cold-hot, sad-happy, good-bad, guilty-innocent and so on. All these are judgments, interpretations based in perception where each apparent separate object has a label or meaning attached to it. These all constitute ways to perpetuate the belief in separation. However, all this is happening within the only mind that exists, within the one that is dreaming the dream. For that reason, for didactic purposes, it could be said that the dreaming mind is non-dual, while the dream is dual. But if the dreaming mind can dream a dream, it is then dual in nature.

In short, it is very simple: all this physical experience is dual by the mere fact that it is governed by opposites, by perception, by what is limited, by a fundamental belief that states "I" am something separate from the rest. It has nothing to do with our Reality. To see Reality is to see that we are That in which this physical experience is contained, in which this dream of separation is contained.

The next chapters will address terms that *A Course in Miracles* employs, since they are part of the foundation of its teaching. As with the word God though, those who feel some resistance to theology can replace terms with ones that are more to their liking. However, I will also suggest that every teaching that points towards Truth is the same, regardless of the terminology employed. Let's start with what is known as *mind, ego and Holy Spirit.*

Mind, Ego and the Holy Spirit

In this chapter we will define three very important terms that form the basis of all the theory and practice shared in this book. These are mind (lowercase), ego and Holy Spirit. Let's start with what is known as mind, or consciousness. Returning to the analogy of the dream, if the body (physical experience) is being dreamed by the mind, then it is not the mind that is in the body, but the opposite. The body (physical experience) is in the mind, in consciousness. However, since this mind of which I speak does not correspond with Reality (uppercase), I will use the following illustration to clarify the reason for distinguishing between the word mind with lowercase and Mind with uppercase:

God
Love
Mind
Reality

The words God, Love, Mind and Reality are synonyms for that which alone is Real. This Truth by itself has no name and no limits; being omnipotent and omnipresent, it simply Is!

Within this Space (God), a thought emerges that is perceived as separate from the Space. This thought is what gives rise to the concept of a Son. That is why it is said that there is the Father (God, the All) and the Son. Only Son! Out of that thought of separation (Son) came what we are going to call mind or consciousness, as can be seen in the next illustration:

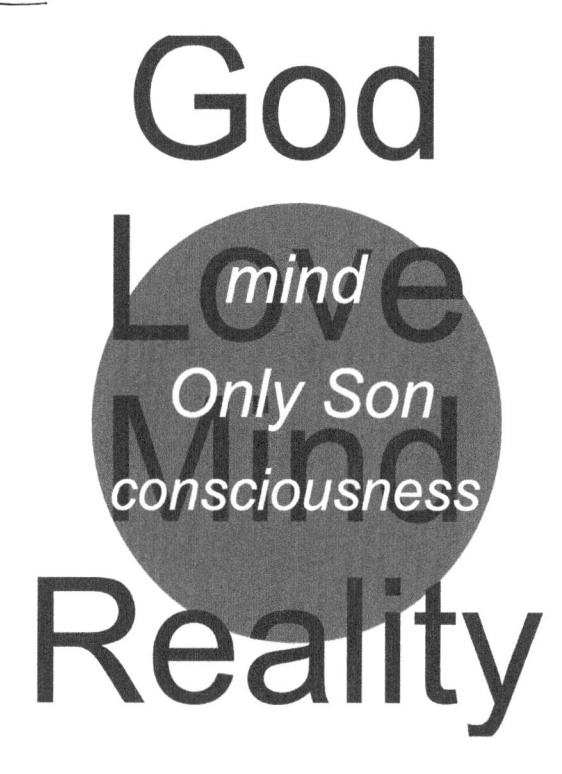

God

Love

Mind

mind
Only Son
consciousness

Reality

In theology, the thought which we are calling here 'mind' (lowercase), where an apparent "separation" is perceived, is known as the fall or original sin. *A Course in Miracles* calls it consciousness because for consciousness to exist, it has to be aware of something (conscious of something). If there were nothing to be conscious of, nothing to be aware of, the only thing that would exist is That which simply Is, That which is One (God, Mind, Love, Reality). So *A Course in Miracles* reminds us: "*Consciousness, the level of perception, was the first split introduced into the mind after the separation, making the mind a perceiver rather than a creator. Consciousness is correctly identified as the domain of the ego. The ego is a wrong-minded attempt to perceive yourself as you wish to be, rather than as you are. Yet you can know yourself only as you are, because that is all you can be sure of. Everything else is open to question*". T-3.IV.2:1-5.

(Note: Since the word consciousness in some doctrines is used to describe God or Truth, and *A Course in Miracles* uses it as the first division that was introduced into the Mind, henceforth, when I use the term "mind" referring to consciousness it will be written in lowercase).

Within the One Mind, that thought (lowercase mind) which was just a meaningless thought, and which never really happened (this will be clarified in the second part under '*common and not so common questions*'), is where the mind appears to "divide" itself into two, into what is known as ego and Holy Spirit. Let's take a look at the following illustration:

God

mind
(Only Son)

ego | Holy Spirit

Love Mind

Reality

The ego is simply a belief in the mind that states that the lowercase mind "exists"; that there was a separation. On the other hand, the Holy Spirit is simply the memory within that same divided mind that knows that the only thing that is real is God, Love, Mind or Reality. *A Course in Miracles* recognizes it as the 'Voice that speaks for God' as stated in the preface: "*When you have been caught in the world of perception you are caught in*

What Happened After Letting God

a dream. You cannot escape without help, because everything your senses show merely witnesses to the reality of the dream. God has provided the Answer, the only Way out, the true Helper. It is the function of His Voice, His Holy Spirit, to mediate between the two worlds. He can do this because, while on the one hand He knows the truth, on the other He also recognizes our illusions, but without believing in them. It is the Holy Spirit's goal to help us escape from the dream world by teaching us how to reverse our thinking and unlearn our mistakes". (Preface UCDM).

I want you to please pay attention to this clarification because although it is very subtle, it is important to grasp in order to avoid confusion. Every time I speak of the Holy Spirit or when I speak of the Voice of the Holy Spirit or His Voice, notice that I use uppercase. I do this because although the Holy Spirit is a memory, a reminder of the Truth that lies within the separated mind, it represents the echo of the Voice of God. Since reference to God always employs uppercase, whenever I refer to the Holy Spirit I will use uppercase. You will also have noticed that when I speak of mind, conscience, and Son, I use the word Son in uppercase. The reason is that within the dream, where there appear to be many, when we speak of God's children, i.e. all of us, we use lowercase. For example right now, the "you" who thinks he is reading these words is as much a son of God as the "me" who believes he is writing them. But "you" as well as "me" are part of the same mind, the same consciousness. Therefore if we speak of "you" or "me", referring to these two "separated" bodies, we use "son" in lowercase. If we speak of the consciousness that dreams us both, we are referring to the Son, the Only Son of God, so the word Son will be written in uppercase.

The separate mind seems to choose between the ego's thought system and the Holy Spirit's as you can see in the following illustration:

God
Love
Mind
Reality

mind
(Only Son)
CHOOSE BETWEEN

ego | Holy Spirit

When the mind (Only Son) chooses, or identifies itself with one thought system, the other is excluded. This being the case, what the ego does is to project itself "out" (something that is in fact impossible because within the mind there is neither "outside" nor "inside"). However, reverting to the dream analogy, the dreamer of the dream believes himself to be in "another place", "outside" of his mind, "outside" of himself, even though the dream that is taking place is happening within his mind, within himself.

In projecting an image, a picture, a world, the ego's thought system causes the mind to remain doubly distracted. First, it is distracted by the belief that it is a mind separate from the Mind, God, Love, Reality and second, because now the divided mind is distracted within itself with the projection of an image, of a dream, as illustrated here:

What Happened After Letting God

God
mind
(Only Son)
CHOOSE BETWEEN
ego | Holy Spirit
Love Mind
Reality

Observe how, in the illustration above, the ego projects an image within the mind where it appears that an "I" is talking with three other people. This is the false "I" projected, the son (lowercase) that I am referring to. Knowing now that when I speak of mind (lowercase) I mean the space in which two completely opposite thought systems appear, the mind can choose which of the two it wants to identify with. And it can only choose one. That is why the Bible talks about not being able to serve two masters: *"No one can serve two masters; because either he will hate one and love the other, or he will cling to one and despise the other. You cannot serve both..."* [Mathew 6:24]. *A Course in Miracles* conveys the same idea: *"... the mind can elect what it chooses to serve. The only limit put on its choice is that it cannot serve two masters"*. T-1.V.5.2-3.

The character's behavior in the dream, meaning "you", "I" and "everyone", is determined by the choice made in the mind, by the mind. If the ego's thought system is chosen, fear is experienced. If on the other hand the Holy Spirit's thought system is chosen, peace will be experienced, regardless of what may be taking place in the dream. That's what *A Course in Miracles* means when it says: "That is why the Bible speaks of *"the peace of God which passeth understanding."* T-2.II.2:9

One is now in a position to ask: "who" or "what" chooses between the two thought systems? This question will leave you running in never-ending circles like a dog chasing its tail. Given that the character "I" has no power of choice, nor power of decision (because again, it is being dreamt), the perceptive consciousness is the one that can make the choice. Instead of attempting to find an answer, why not ask yourself the following question instead: did you personally choose to wake up this morning or was it something that happened? And I'm not talking about setting the alarm clock to wake you up at a specific time. I'm talking about the experience itself of waking up. You could say it was God's Will. You could say it was consciousness or destiny, or you could simply say (and this would be in my view a far more accurate answer) "I don't know!" I want you to be open to the possibility that if you do not know what made this event happen, then we'll have to recognize that we do not know anything about what happens or why. But one thing we can be certain of is that when something happens, if all personal interpretations are set aside, peace is what is experienced. Could we agree on that? And if you find yourself reading this kind of material, it could be said that at some level, the mind is now choosing a thought system that is more in alignment with Truth, with Love, with God.

Continuing then, if the Holy Spirit's thought system is chosen by the mind through the practice of true forgiveness, *A Course in Miracles* teaches that, little by little, the mind will be reminded of its Reality as God, as Love, as Truth. This will be a very kind and loving process: *"If you are willing to renounce the role of guardian of your thought system and open it to me, I will correct it very gently and lead you back to God".* T-4.I.4: 7.

The next term I am going to share, the fundamental basis for

What Happened After Letting God

this dream of separation to be sustained, is what is known as *"unconscious guilt"*.

Unconscious Guilt

Unconscious guilt underlies all the fear we experience, according to *A Course in Miracles*. In fact the Course sees it as the guilt we feel for having "separated", or rather for believing that we have separated, from God. But for people who are not familiar with the Course's teachings, I will first use a dual analogy in an attempt to illustrate how, apparently, this unconscious guilt originated in the mind, and to also integrate the terms ego, Holy Spirit and God. One last thing, in the analogy, where the 'father' is synonymous with God and 'mother' synonymous with the Holy Spirit, I will keep the word father and mother in lowercase, whereas any reference to God and the Holy Spirit will appear in uppercase.

Imagine being at home (in the Kingdom where everything is One). A glass falls from your hands and breaks. You observe the experience with complete innocence: nothing happened! However, your neighbor (ego) runs out of his house after hearing the sound of the broken glass and shouts: "LOOK WHAT YOU HAVE DONE?" At that moment you feel scared. Your neighbor now tells you: "WHAT YOU DID IS BAD, YOU SHOULD BE ASHAMED OF YOURSELF." Guilt is generated in you for having done something which in itself does not mean anything, it's just a broken glass. The Course puts it this way: " *Into eternity, where all is one, there crept a tiny, mad idea, at which the Son of God remembered not to laugh.*" T-27.VIII.6: 2. But you feel that what has happened is something "bad", something "wrong", just because you believed what your neighbor told you. Worse still, not only what happened was "bad", but now you think that "you" are "bad" (you are guilty).

Then he yells at you: "WHEN YOUR FATHER (God) COMES HOME YOU WILL BE PUNISHED!" *You feel completely terrified and don't know where to tur*n. You would normally seek help from your father but according to your neighbor, your father is the one who is going to punish you. Therefore you now fear your father (you fear God). Your neighbor, the very one who filled your head with fear, now wants to play the role of your "savior", advising you to go to your room, get into bed and hide under the blanket. There your neighbor will "protect" you from your father. As you can see, now you believe that your neighbor (ego) is the "good guy", and your father (God) is the "bad guy". And because you are so frightened in your room, you cling to your teddy bear in a desperate bid for security.

Your father (God) arrives home with a strong desire to give his son (you, the Holy and Innocent Son of God) a kiss and a big hug. However you fear your father, not because he is going to punish you, but because you have believed the story that your neighbor told you about him. Your father sends your mother (Holy Spirit) to look for you so that he can give you that hug and that kiss. However you do not trust your mother because you think it's a trap that your father has set so that when you come out he can punish you. Even so, your mom very gently talks to you. She asks you what's wrong with you and you respond by saying that your father is going to punish you for breaking the glass. Then she asks you why you think this. You tell her it's because your neighbor told you so. She very lovingly tells you to trust her and not to listen to your neighbor.

However, because you feel so afraid for having believed your neighbor's lie, it will take you a while before you feel comfortable enough to trust your mother. *A Course in Miracles* states it this way: "*You have very little trust in me* ("me" for the purposes of *A Course in Miracles* would be Holy Spirit, Inner Teacher, Jesus or however you want to name it) *as yet, but it will increase as you turn more and more often to me instead of to your ego for guidance. The results will convince you increasingly that this choice is the only sane one you can make*". T-4.VI.3:1-2. In other words, as you feel the peace that comes from listening to your mother's words, your confidence in her grows. This is the result the Course is referring to; the peace that is experienced when the mind chooses the Holy Spirit's thought system.

Firmly holding on to your mother's hand, although a little gingerly because you still experience fear, you walk with her towards the door. *A Course in Miracles* says: "*Try to pass the clouds by whatever means appeals to you. If it helps you, think of me holding your hand and leading you. And I assure you this will be no idle fantasy*". W-pI.70.9: 2-4. Your neighbor, however, seeing that his lie is going to be discovered, shouts at you and urges you not to go with your mother. This is why the Course reminds us: "*The ego is deceived by everything you do, especially when you respond to the Holy Spirit, because at such times its confusion increases. The ego is, therefore, particularly likely to attack you when you react lovingly, because it has evaluated you as unloving and you are going against its judgment. The ego will attack your motives as soon as they become clearly out of accord with its perception of you. This is when it will shift abruptly from suspiciousness to viciousness, since its uncertainty is increased. Yet it is surely pointless to attack in return. What can this mean except that you are agreeing with the ego's evaluation of what you are?*" T-9.VII.4:4-9.

Trusting your mother, you begin to walk with her towards the door, even when your neighbor tries to persuade you not to. During this period you have to keep your focus on your mother and nothing else. If you don't, you will experience confusion, since you do not know who to pay attention to: your neighbor (the fear that seems so real); or your mother (the Voice of Love, which, although it is your natural inheritance, you still feel unworthy of receiving). The Course talks about this period when it says: "*And now you stand in terror before what you swore never to look upon. Your eyes look down, remembering your promise to your "friends." The "loveliness" of sin, the delicate appeal of guilt, the "holy" waxen image of death, and the fear of vengeance of the ego you swore in blood not to desert, all rise and bid you not to raise your eyes. For you realize that if you look on this and let the veil be lifted, they will be gone forever. All of your "friends," your "protectors" and your "home" will vanish. Nothing that you remember now will you remember*". T-19.IV.D.6:1-6.

By the way, 'coming out of the room' is another way of saying 'waking up from the dream'. Although I used the example of your neighbor as the reason you do not want to leave the room, the teddy bear you love so much is also a distraction. The difference is, your neighbor employs fear to keep you in the room, while you use your teddy bear to avoid facing the fear of leaving the room by convincing yourself that, with the teddy bear, the room is a good place to be. (This theme will be developed in the next chapter).

Continuing with the story, regardless of the fear or the confusion that you may be experiencing, you keep holding on to your mother's hand until you walk out the door. Then your father comes to you with his arms wide open and gives you a big hug, telling you how much he adores you. In that instant all your fear disappears and you begin to laugh at the silliness of the story you bought into.

Let's see how this analogy applies to our physical experience. This world in which I appear to be, this body that appears to be my identity, are part of the room in which I hide for fear of God's punishment. In an attempt to hide my feelings of guilt and do everything possible not to feel them, or at least feel them as little as possible, I fill myself with teddy bears (distractions and entertainment). As the course reminds us: "*Your faith is placed in the most trivial and insane symbols; pills, money, "protective" clothing, influence, prestige, being liked, knowing the "right" people, and an endless list of forms of nothingness that you endow with magical powers. All these things are your replacements for the Love of God (the Real World). All these things are cherished to ensure a body identification. They are songs of praise to the ego. Do not put your faith in the worthless. It will not sustain you*". W-pI.50.1: 3..2: 1-5. This is how we try to make the dream more bearable.

So I feel guilty for having "left" Home, and to avoid feeling it I hide myself, projecting the dream, my new "home". But no matter how hard I try to make this dream my home, it is not possible, because as the Course reminds us: "*This world you seem to live in is not home to you. And somewhere in your mind you know that this is true"*. W-pI.182.1: 1-2. *How could I live in this world and feel at Home when my Home is complete bliss, infinite peace, perfect love, unlimited abundance? A Course in Miracles asks: "Can you imagine what a state of mind without illusions is? How it would feel? Try to remember when there was a time - perhaps a minute, maybe even less - when nothing came to interrupt your peace; when you were certain you were loved and safe. Then try to picture what it would be like to have that moment be extended to the end of time and to eternity. Then let the sense of quiet that you felt be multiplied a hundred times, and then be multiplied another hundred more. And now you have a hint, not more than just the faintest intimation of the state your mind will rest in when the truth has come. Without illusions* (without the dream) *there could be no fear, no doubt and no attack. When truth has come all pain is over, for there is no room for transitory thoughts and dead ideas to linger in your mind"*. W-pI.107.2: 2-5..3:1-3.

The interesting thing is that all the conflict (unconscious guilt) can be eradicated immediately with a simple change of mind. Yet despite intellectual understanding, the dream, which is the limitation imposed on to the Totality, is maintained. The mind keeps choosing the dream because of the laws that the mind projects onto the dreamed character. These laws which the dreamed character is governed by and in which it firmly believes, are what drives the dreamed character to continue to hold on to its illusory "personal" identity: **the avoidance of pain and the pursuit of pleasure.**

The Avoidance of Pain and The Pursuit of Pleasure.

The ego's thought system, or fear, wants to maintain the distracted mind by keeping its attention on the dream, making it believe that it is a body rather than a mind that is dreaming a body. It does so through what is experienced as bodily perceptions and bodily sensations. For example, when "I" (the body that I now believe myself to be) listen to something, it appears as if there is an "I" that is listening. I have forgotten that it is the mind that dreams this "I" who experiences "listening". When "I" see something, it appears as if there is an "I" that is seeing, forgetting that it is the mind that dreams this "I" who experiences "seeing". When "I" feel something, it appears as if there is an "I" that is feeling, forgetting that it is the mind that dreams this "I" who experiences "feeling". However when I let go of all personal interpretations (let go of my belief system) even for a moment, attention ceases to be in what the mind perceives as a "separate entity" (the "individual" body "separate" from everything) and a sense of peace settles in.

This peace is a subtle memory of the mind's natural state. The awareness always remains, regardless of whether we've forgotten it. If this state of mind were sustained for a long time, the world of perception, this physical experience, would lose all its attraction and the dream would disappear. *A Course in Miracles* says: *"All worldly states must be illusory. If God were reached directly in sustained awareness, the body would not be long maintained".* M-26.3:7-8.

While the mind remains distracted by putting all its attention on the dream, believing that it is a body, the senses "pretend" to report to the mind what the "body" is "perceiving", "feeling" or "sensing" without realizing that it is the mind itself that projects onto the body what the body thinks it is feeling or perceiving. That is why *A Course in Miracles* reminds us: *"It is your mind*

What Happened After Letting God

(not the brain or whatever we think is located in the body's head, but the mind that dreams the dream) *which gave the body all the functions that you see in it, and set its value far beyond a little pile of dust and water."* W- pI.135.6:4. Now the mind, through the character "I", believes that it is a body that can feel and every bodily sensation is interpreted in one of two ways, as painful or pleasurable. That is why, within this apparent physical experience, the human being is constantly avoiding pain and seeking pleasure. Actually, both are sensations that do not mean anything but the chosen interpretation will dictate whether the character "I" suffers or not.

I want to emphasize that attachment to the dream is intensified by what we apparently "feel". We can do all kinds of meditative practices and remain silent, but when a feeling is experienced, it is practically impossible to ignore. This reminds me of an excerpt from the Course that tells us: *"The body is merely part of your experience in the physical world. Its abilities can be and frequently are overevaluated. However, it is almost impossible to deny its existence in this world."* T-2.IV.3: 8-10.

So when the mind interprets a feeling or an experience as painful, it looks for ways to feel better (by seeking pleasure). I call it the help-seeking mode. In my experience, this seeking of help happens in three stages, from complete unconsciousness to becoming conscious. It could also happen as an instantaneous moment of awareness. But generally in my experience it happens as follows:

First stage: This is when you are completely unconscious, believing that your "reality" is this physical experience and therefore the help you seek is aimed at feeling better within the dream.

Second stage: Once you try to seek help within the context of the dream, in this world, but the feeling of lack or suffering continues, this is usually when you begin to explore the "spiritual" path (you become a seeker). I put the word spiritual in quotes because contemporary spirituality, believe it or not, is still a part of the ego since it is still associated with the dream. This is when fear (ego) uses the same spirituality and disguises it with pleasurable experiences for the dream to continue to be appealing. At least this new approach opens the mind to the exploration of new paths and practices such as meditation and contemplation, leading to the recognition that our reality is something beyond a body, beyond a physical experience.

One thing I would like to mention before continuing is that meditation, especially at the beginning, can become a subtle way of escaping because the mind still believes in the "reality" of the dream. Such meditation at best allows the mind to have temporary experiences of "peace". Peace is in quotes because the real peace of which I am speaking is a permanent, not a temporary state. To give you an example, when a soldier is in the middle of a war and the two sides run out of ammunition, that period of reload, even if there is no shooting and it looks "quiet," is still part of the war. It is only a matter of time before the shooting continues. Same with meditation. It can be a sudden escape where the mind is in a temporary state of quietude. But once the mind comes out of the meditation, all fears are once again ready to arise. In the section entitled 'common and not so common questions', this subject of meditation will be addressed in more detail. So, oscillating between pleasure and pain is how this character "I" (this body that appears to be real), reacts to the dream as if the dream were a part of its "reality". The dream, being the ego's invention to keep the mind distracted from Truth, distracted from itself, contains fear disguised in many forms. *A Course in Miracles* explains: "*The dreams you think you like would hold you back as much as those in which the fear is seen. For every dream is but a dream of fear, no matter what the form it seems to take. The fear is seen within, without, or both. Or it can be disguised in pleasant form. But never is it absent from the dream, for fear is the material of dreams, from which they all are made*". T-29. IV.2: 1-5.

But pleasure as well as pain are simply two sides of the same coin. As long as we keep holding on to the belief that we are bodies, separate entities, these two emotions, states, sensations or whatever we choose to call them will continue to run our lives, making the attainment of inner peace an impossibility. That's why *A Course in Miracles* states: *"Sin shifts from pain to pleasure, and again to pain. For either witness is the same, and carries but one message: "You are here, within this body, and you can be hurt. You can have pleasure, too, but only at the cost of pain. These witnesses are joined by many more. Each one seems different because it has a different name, and so it seems to answer to a different sound. Except for this, the witnesses of sin are all alike. Call pleasure pain, and it will hurt. Call pain a pleasure, and the pain behind the pleasure will be felt no more. Sin's witnesses but shift from name to name, as one steps forward and another back"*. T-27.VI.2: 1-9.

Third stage: This begins when you are becoming aware that you are the dreamer of the dream. It tends to be a rather unstable period because although you know that the world has nothing to offer (given the fact that you are starting to become aware of Who or What you are), this awareness is not fully established in the mind. The world still has a strong appeal and you are not ready to fully let it go. As stated before in this book, Course in Miracles explains: *"As this recognition becomes more firmly established, it becomes a turning point. This ultimately reawakens spiritual vision, simultaneously weakening the investment in physical sight. The alternating investment in the two levels of perception is usually experienced as conflict, which can become very acute. But the outcome is as certain as God"*. T-2.III.3:7-10.

While the physical experience oscillates between pain and pleasure, the distractions are inevitable. The question that arises now is how one can prevent oneself from being distracted by this dream, especially when feelings and sensations seem to trap us. The answer is through the practice known as *true forgiveness*.

True Forgiveness

There is a fundamental reason why this chapter is entitled 'true forgiveness'. While my previous book included a chapter bearing the same title, I would like to elaborate a little on this subject from a deeper understanding. Again, emphasizing the fact that A Course in Miracles is a purely non-dual teaching, in this world of perceived separation, we have learned that forgiveness is an act that takes place between different people. Using the interaction between two as an example, one person is the victim and the other is the victimizer. Therefore the victim "forgives" the victimizer.

However to return to the dream analogy where the projected physical experience is taking place, in the only dreaming mind that there is, the victim and the victimizer are part of the same mind. So it does not matter which part of the mind plays the role of victim and which part of the mind plays the role of victimizer. Since the mind is interacting with itself, it is the mind that attacks itself and simultaneously "forgives" itself. Becoming aware that the dream is a projection means realizing that it matters not what takes place within the dream; nothing can affect the mind that dreams it at all. Given this to be the case, is it necessary to forgive? The answer is obvious. It is not because in reality nothing is happening! Hence this excerpt from A Course in Miracles: "Forgiveness recognizes what you thought your brother did to you has not occurred. It does not pardon sins and make them real. It sees there was no sin. And in that view are all your sins forgiven". W-pII.1.1: 1-4.

We always have to bear in mind that A Course in Miracles speaks to us on two levels simultaneously. There is the level of form or physical experience, which we take to be our "reality" and the level of the mind, which has to do with the message that goes to the mind that dreams the dream. Therefore as long as I am identified with the "I" that I take myself to be i.e. the physical body, people will be perceived as doing things to "others", even doing things to "me" as well as "I" to "them." But if I am aware that this world is a projection, an illusion, forgiveness means remembering what I really Am.

Before continuing, let's briefly define an illusion. An illusion is something that is perceived as real but it is not what it appears to be. For example, on a cinema screen the images are perceived as real. They seem to have shape, volume and depth, but in reality the only thing that is real is a flat blank screen upon which the images are being projected. This physical experience is also perceived as very real, very "solid". Yet it is not what it appears to be. It is in fact a projection of the mind that dreams this dream. In that sense it is illusory. But because our experience gives testimony to its apparent "reality", an internal change in perception must take place so that the awareness of its illusory nature can be accepted, not as a mere concept, but as an unquestionable fact. This is what the words and concepts shared in this book point to. Indeed the teachings of *A Course in Miracles* and any other non-dual philosophy point to this same phenomenon. This subject will be explored further in the section 'common and not so common questions'.

To continue, the Course employs the word forgiveness in a very special way. On a surface level, the word forgiveness seems to have a "benevolent" intention. Yet if we look closely, it sustains the belief in guilt, the belief in separation, the context that perpetuates a sense of guilt and fear. *A Course in Miracles* uses it to restore its true function, to see that there is nothing to forgive, which is to eradicate any sense of guilt or fear so that inner peace can be restored in the mind.

Let us remember that in order to forgive, we must first judge. This idea of judgment is supported by the belief that God judges. So in a way, holding on to this belief is what gives us the "right" to judge others as well as ourselves in His name. In addition, however much we believe that forgiving in the conventional way is doing the "right thing", in reality what

True Forgiveness

we succeed in doing is increasing internal guilt, justifying our belief in separation. But when we become aware that we are one mind, we see that we are judging ourselves and so we are the ones who will experience the pain of that judgment. In the application of true forgiveness we feel better, not because we have done the "right" thing, but because we are the only ones that are being forgiven. That is why the Course reminds us: "It can be but myself I crucify: When this is firmly understood and kept in full awareness, you will not attempt to harm yourself, nor make your body slave to vengeance. You will not attack yourself, and you will realize that to attack another is but to attack yourself. You will be free of the insane belief that to attack a brother saves yourself. And you will understand his safety is your own, and in his healing you are healed". W-pI.196.1:1-4.

True forgiveness then, the objective of which is to return the mind to its natural state of union, of peace, is embraced when all personal interpretation is put aside. This is especially true when the idea that there is something or someone outside to "forgive" is abandoned.

The practice of forgiveness can be summarised as follows:

1. When I am presented with something in my field of conscious awareness that triggers any kind of discomfort, I realize that I have been given an opportunity to practice forgiveness. I call this "the signal".

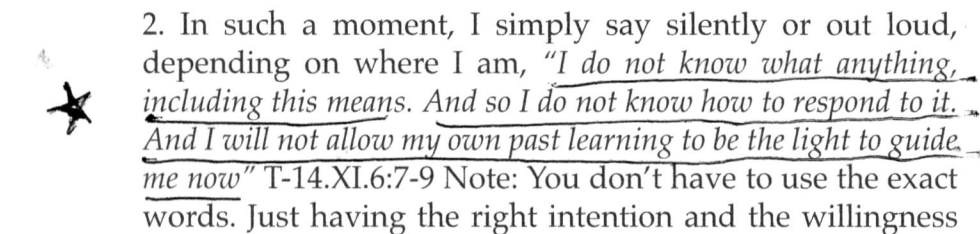

2. In such a moment, I simply say silently or out loud, depending on where I am, "*I do not know what anything, including this means. And so I do not know how to respond to it. And I will not allow my own past learning to be the light to guide me now*" T-14.XI.6:7-9 Note: You don't have to use the exact words. Just having the right intention and the willingness to relinquish your thoughts, ideas and beliefs to the Holy Spirit is all that matters.

3. I make peace my number one priority while trusting that the Holy Spirit is doing the work. (This makes steps 2 and 3

What Happened After Letting God

interchangeable).

Although these three fundamental steps, as outlined in my previous book do not change, I will elaborate on each one of them based on the deepening of my understanding and application of *A Course in Miracles'* teachings since I started practising them more than 10 years ago.

1. When I am presented with something in my field of conscious awareness that triggers any kind of discomfort, I realize that I have been given an opportunity to practice forgiveness. I call this "the signal".

When I say "...*something in my field of conscious awareness that triggers any kind of discomfort*", meaning, whenever our experience of our thoughts or outside circumstances and events rests on our personal interpretations, a loss of peace is experienced. While all experiences, thoughts, events and circumstances are in and of themselves neutral, our conditioning divides them into two categories; painful ones including any sensations we want to avoid, and pleasurable ones for which every human being seeks. If you did not feel any kind of painful physical sensation, you would not perceive anything as a problem. The result would be no loss of peace. Can we agree on that? All interpretations stem from the thought system the mind choose in each present moment. When identified with the thought system of the Holy Spirit (Right Mind, Inner Wisdom, etc.), His interpretation alone will prevail over any thought or circumstance that may arise and lead to an experience of peace. Conversely when identified with the ego's thought system (personal interpretation based on our beliefs), the same thought or circumstance will result in pain. The first step, then, is to recognize the thought system with which I am identified. With the deepening of my comprehension of *A Course in Miracles'* non-dual teaching has come the realization that if I try to apply true forgiveness only when things go "wrong" (ignoring the genuine desire for Truth, the genuine desire to remember what I really Am), then my adherence to believing myself to be a body is mentally reinforced. Instead of applying the practice of true forgiveness to remember who I am, it can be seen how the ego mind twists it into applying forgiveness to project a "better" version of my character. Daily contemplative practices allowed me to observe the ease with which the mind distracts itself so that each experience, "positive" or "negative", can be now employed for the remembrance of the reality that I Am. That's what I call living consciously. Living in this way is the equivalent of integrating the three steps into one. But since there is such a deep identification with this "I", this "person" I believe myself to be, I must begin by observing the events that I judge to be the "cause" of my loss of peace, and this very awareness will bring me naturally to the second step.

2. At this stage, I simply say silently or out loud, depending on where I am, "I do not know what anything, including this means. And so I do not know how to respond to it. And I will not allow my own past learning to be the light to guide me now." T-14.XI.6:7-9.

Remember that the accuracy of the words is not the important thing. Simply having the right intention and the willingness to relinquish your thoughts, ideas and beliefs to the Holy Spirit will suffice.

Becoming aware that *A Course in Miracles* is a purely non-dual teaching has meant becoming aware of my ongoing identification with a personal "I" when I write . This is the distinction that moved me to write this book. Instead of using words, this second step calls for us to simply put aside all kinds of personal interpretations. Whatever we feel, whatever we think, all that is observed, whatever story the mind wants to fabricate is released. In that sense, these excerpts from the Course serve to support this second step: "*Forgiveness, on the other hand, is still, and quietly does nothing. It offends no aspect of reality, nor seeks to twist it to appearances it likes. It merely looks, and waits, and judges not*". W-pII.1.4: 1-3. Or: "*The miracle comes quietly into the mind that stops an instant and is still*". T-28.I.11:1. As we can see

What Happened After Letting God   43

in the first and second steps, it is a matter of opening myself to a complete acceptance of the present moment, a complete acceptance of what is, being aware that my genuine desire is for inner peace, the peace of God. If the intention is for anything other than Truth or, as I mentioned earlier, to change anything within the dream, to make a "better version" of the person I think I am, it is not the peace of God that I truly desire. It is rather an exchange of illusions. That's how the ego's thought system keeps the mind distracted, focusing its attention on the dream. But when there is a true desire for Truth, life will lead us down a path, as well as towards any resource that supports this intention so that our desire can be fulfilled.

What now remains is the third step.

3. I make peace my number one priority while trusting that the Holy Spirit is doing the work.

The "letting go" of which I spoke is what took place in the second step. The difference with the third step is that it is not taken by us. It is the correction that the Holy Spirit makes. As we deepen in the practice of true forgiveness, the experience that naturally takes place is of inner peace because, although the mind still perceives the world of dreams, it does not feel affected by them. That is why lesson 155 of *A Course in Miracles* reminds us: *"There is a way of living in the world that is not here, although it seems to be. You do not change appearance, though you smile more frequently. Your forehead is serene; your eyes are quiet. And the ones who walk the world as you do recognize their own. Yet those who have not yet perceived the way will recognize you also, and believe that you are like them, as you were before"*. W-pI.155.1: 1-5.

The term that *A Course in Miracles* uses to describe this stage is known as *"the happy dream"* (T-18). The mind is still dreaming but, being aware that it is a dream, it is becoming ready to release it and awaken to its Reality as God. *A Course in Miracles* states it this way: *"Prepare you now for the undoing of what never was. If you already understood the difference between truth and illusion... the Holy Spirit's teaching, and all the means by which salvation is accomplished, would have no purpose. For they are all but aspects of the plan to change your dreams of fear to happy dreams, from which you waken easily to knowledge"*. T-18.V.1:1-2..3-4.

The three steps I have just shared about the practice of forgiveness are summarized as follows:

1. Become aware / realize that you are not at peace.

2. Release your personal interpretations.

3. The correction - this step is taken by the Holy Spirit.

In the *common and not so common questions* below, doubts and concerns about the practice and application of true forgiveness will be addressed. We will also observe how subtly the ego's thought system (fear) tries to hold on to its identity by attempting to misinterpret the Course's non-dual message. That is why we are reminded in *A Course in Miracles*: *"I have made every effort to use words that are almost impossible to distort, but it is always possible to twist symbols around if you wish"*. T-3.I.3: 11.

Common and Not So Common Questions

In my experience, while reading a lot of theory about anything serves to support our intellectual understanding, I have noticed that when there is a lot of mental resistance the message ends up diluted, distorted or simply not understood. In the same way that a magician distracts his spectators to perform his trick, mental comments and questions do exactly the same thing. In other words, if the mind focuses on trying to understand something that can only be experienced, it becomes so frustrated or stressed that it overlooks the obvious message. But when the mind relaxes, understanding comes when you least expect it.

The objective of the rest of this book, where random questions are answered, is to bring the mind to a state of curiosity where understanding can take place without the need for inquiry or mental effort. If any inquiry becomes necessary, it will happen very organically, so there are no rules to follow. Even answers that may be completely irrelevant to our personal experience can serve as a catalyst for the emergence of understanding. You will also realize that practically all the answers seem to be repetitive because the Truth is One, it is Absolute. Although the ego's thought system asks countless questions in so many different ways, the answer is always the same, pointing to the same place.

So enjoy the rest of this book, fully trusting that if there is an answer that may be useful in your process, it will be revealed. An open mind is the only thing that is required. And since the main focus of this book is intertwined with the teachings of *A Course in Miracles*, let's start with the following question:

1 How did A Course in Miracles originate?

The scribe of the Course was a doctor of psychology called Helen Schucman. The material was channeled through her. The detailed explanation can be found in the preface of *A Course in Miracles*, not because it is important, but because many people have asked about it. That is why the preface of the Course says: *"The names of the collaborators in the recording of the Course do not appear on the cover because the Course can and should stand on its own. It is not intended to become the basis for another cult. Its only purpose is to provide a way in which some people will be able to find their own Internal Teacher"*. (Preface UCDM).

However, to maintain the non-dual essence of the message that I want to share through this book, I will address that same question from another angle. When a sleeping mind is dreaming, all its attention is directed towards the images in the dream. Therefore within the dream another symbol is projected, another illusion so to speak, that for the purposes of this example has the form of a book full of words, whose sole purpose is to lead the mind to stop paying attention to the dream so that it can be made aware of its Reality as the dreamer of the dream.

Speaking at the level "we" as human beings appear to be, if I told you that the book '*A Course in Miracles*' appeared out of nowhere, you would take me for a madman and would not even open yourself up to its message. While the fact that a woman named Helen Schucman was the scribe of the material is totally irrelevant, at least it serves to identify some origin for the book. From the point of view of there being only one mind, and we are all a part of that same mind, it might be deduced that the book was written by all of us. What is really important is not the story of how the material originated, but whether through practice one can experience the effect of its message, which is inner peace.

2 Why is the Course so difficult to understand?

A Course in Miracles is very simple to understand when the mind is clear and there is no confusion in levels. That is why the text reminds us: *"To you who seem to find this Course to be too difficult to learn, let me repeat that to achieve a goal you must proceed in its direction, not away from it. And every road that leads the other way will not advance the purpose to be found. If this be difficult to understand, then is this Course impossible to learn. But only then. For otherwise, it is a simple teaching in the obvious"*. T-31.IV.7: 3-7.

What happens is that as long as there is identification with a personal "I", as long as there is a strong identification with myself as a "person", the fear of letting go of that identity (letting go of the attachment to the dream) will not allow the mind to accept the simplicity of this message. If you accept the Course´s proposal, that the personal "I" is sustained by the fundamental belief that says "I exist as a human being in this world separated from everything", this sense of "I" would disappear. Another way of saying it, "it would die." This generates fear, which is why the ego´s thought system distorts the message in an attempt to adapt it to its distorted interpretation. As previously noted, this is why the Course reminds us: *"I have made every effort to use words that are almost impossible to distort, but it is always possible to twist symbols around if you wish"*. T-3.I.3: 11.

The Course is a practical mind training: *"This Course is always practical"* (M-16.4:1) and it begins with bringing the mind back to peace while the mind is still dreaming (identified with this personal "I"). Then, when the mind is ready, it will let go of the attachment to the dream before it is finally ready to let it go all together. That is why the Course reminds us: *"The Holy Spirit, ever practical in His wisdom, accepts your dreams and uses them as means for waking. You would have used them to remain asleep. I said before that the first change, before dreams disappear, is that your dreams of fear are changed to happy dreams"*. T-18.II.6: 1-3.

The Course speaks to the mind that is dreaming "us" without frightening it. It does so on two levels: as a mind and as if we were the "I" character that listens to its words. Specifically, while the mind that dreams the dream is identified with the character in the dream, the Course's message within the dream appears to be directed to the character in the dream, yet in reality it is directed to the mind that is dreaming the character in the dream. The Course needs to employ language, using those symbols and concepts with which the character in the dream is familiar. For this reason, the Course's message can sometimes appear to be contradictory, because on the one hand it says: *"There is no world! This is the central thought the Course attempts to teach"*. W-pI.132.6: 2-3 and simultaneously it says: *"Those who would let illusions be lifted from their minds are this world's saviors, walking the world with their Redeemer, and carrying His message of hope and freedom and release from suffering to everyone who needs a miracle to save him"*. T-22.IV.6: 5.

On one hand the Course says: *"God did not make the body, because it is destructible, and therefore not of the Kingdom. The body is the symbol of what you think you are. It is clearly a separation device, and therefore does not exist"*. T-6.V.A.2:1-3. On the other says: *"The body cannot heal, because it cannot make itself sick. It needs no healing. Its health or sickness depends entirely on how the mind perceives it, and the purpose that the mind would use it for"*. T-19.I.3: 1-3.

So does the world exist or not? Does the body exist or not? When you are aware, again, that the Course is speaking to the dreaming mind, the mind that is dreaming "you", "me", "everyone", the "world" and not to the "I" character, reading the text becomes very clear as nothing is taken out of context. I am going to use the examples I shared so you can see how simple the Course's message is once it is not taken out of context:

"Those who would let illusions be lifted from their minds are this world's saviors, walking the world with their Redeemer, and carrying His message of hope and freedom and release from suffering to everyone who needs a miracle to save him". T-22.IV.6: 5.

A sleeping person does not realize that everything that takes place in his dream is part of the content of his mind. When the person (dreamer) becomes aware that he is dreaming (lucid dreaming), he observes all the content of his mind releasing itself, becomes full of hope and experiences complete emancipation from all suffering. In the dream, the mind seems to see "others". Interacting with them reminds the mind that it is dreaming. This is how "he" becomes the savior of "the world" (the savior of his mind) because there is no world! For example, right this moment, there appears to be a "you" who is reading these words, and there appears to be an "I" who has written them and this is the context that the mind that dreams us both uses to awaken itself. It seems that there is an "I" carrying messages of hope, freedom, emancipation of suffering to everyone (in this case "you"), when in fact the message is only for myself, because there is only One of "us" (One Mind). Since "you" and "I" are a fragment of the same mind, this is a circular process that does not take place between "two" ("you" and "I"), but takes place between the mind itself.

Let's look at the second example: *"The body cannot heal, because it cannot make itself sick. It needs no healing. Its health or sickness depends entirely on how the mind perceives it, and the purpose that the mind would use it for"*. T-19.I.3: 1-3.

The body cannot be cured or cause illnesses to itself, not because the body "exists", but because it is an image projected by the mind. Images in a dream have no "causative" power, they cannot make decisions nor feel anything. They are only images that behave according to the dictates of the mind that dreams them. The Course is not based on doing anything special about the body or assuming that if you change your mentality the body can be "cured". The Course simply emphasizes that everything that takes place in the dream is caused by the dreaming mind. Following the practice of true forgiveness, when the mind identifies with the Holy Spirit's thought system, the body (projected image) may, or may not experience some physical conditions that are usually associated with a mind filled with fear. Either way, a sick body or a "healthy" body, the body

Re: "Death" of the body

will "die" since the dream cannot continue on eternally. The difference is, when the time comes to let go of the body, a mind ★ free of guilt releases it peacefully, without any sense of suffering because the mind, being consciously aware that everything is a dream, desires only the experience of true freedom, the experience of permanent inner peace and happiness that takes place when the identification with the body ceases. Then, when ★ the time comes, according to the script, the body is ready to be released, and this last step is not taken by "us" (the body) but by God, as the Course reminds us: "*I have said that the last step in the reawakening to knowledge is given by God.*" T-7.I-6: 3.

Again, since the Course uses the same language and symbols with which the figures in the dream are familiar, then little by little and very lovingly, the message of the Course brings the mind's attention from the dream, to the mind that dreams the dream, making it aware that its true nature is a dreaming mind and not a separate body. The perfection of the curriculum of *A Course in Miracles* (which by the way, is highly individualized) as the desire for peace increases the identification with the "I", the desire for the dream world diminishes. The simplicity of the Course's message then will be welcomed without any fear because there is no fear of losing one's false sense of identity. The mind is clear that it is Mind (Love, God) not a "separate ★ entity (physical body)".

3 Who is the Son of God?

The Son of God is actually "all of us", and yet, there is only One. In other words, the Only Son of God is that part of the Whole that believes it has separated itself from the Whole. It is referred to as mind or conscience as I explained in the chapter entitled 'Mind, Ego and The Holy Spirit'. Let us always remember the difference between the Son of God (Son in uppercase) and the

sp. Consciousness

son of God (son in lowercase). Let's review part of what was shared in that chapter using the following images:

God
Love
mind
Mind
Only Son
consciousness
Reality

Within the Mind (uppercase), call it God, Love, Mind, Reality, etc., where there appears to be a separation, this thought of separation is known as the Son, the Only Son. This is the original thought that in contemporary theology is also known as the fall or original sin. (In another question we will define what is known as "sin" according to the teachings of *A Course in Miracles*).

It is within this "separate" mind (consciousness) that a dream is projected. In the dream, where the appearance of many bodies seems to take place, all of the bodies are together known as the "children of God." So when the Course is talking about the images projected in the dream, it addresses them as the son of God (lowercase) as we see in the following image:

What Happened After Letting God

When *A Course in Miracles* talks about the Son of God (uppercase), it is referring to me as mind, as consciousness. When the Course talks about the son of God (lowercase) it is referring to me as a separate character in the dream.

4 What is sin?

The moment the mind believes that it has separated from Itself, this is what is known as a sin. The Course, however, uses the word sin instead of separation because in theology, since this term is used to perpetuate guilt and fear, the Course now uses it to take away all that weight by restoring Jesus' message of love. That is why the Course says: *"Darkness is lack of light as sin is lack of love"* (T-1.IV.3: 1) and *"Since love is all there is, sin in the sight of the Holy Spirit is a mistake to be corrected, rather than an evil to be punished"*. (Preface UCDM). The error that is being discussed here and therefore needs correction, is the error of believing that I am a body living in a world of separation (dream) rather than what I really am: Mind, Love, God, Reality. That is all.

5 What is the miracle?

From the dual perspective, the miracle is a change that defies logical explanation, which takes place within the dream. A disease might be spontaneously eradicated or missing money and resources may appear unexpectedly. I had no work and then "coincidentally" someone calls and offers me a job. The fulfillment of a desire for someone to change her mind or for something in the world to change or a need to be fulfilled may all appear to be "miraculous" events. Yet they are in fact exchanges of illusions. That's why *A Course in Miracles* says: *"The healing of effect without the cause can merely shift effects to other forms. And this is not release"*. T-26.VII.14: 2-3.

Let's look at this extract adding parentheses: *"The healing of effect* (whatever is perceived in the world of illusions as a change) *without the cause* (remembering that I am a mind projecting a dream) *can merely shift effects to other forms* (a change in the dream can take place, which could have the appearance of a "resolution" of the apparent problem). *And this is not release"* (it is not release [liberation] because the mind is still dreaming).

The miracle we are talking about takes place when fear is replaced by love, regardless of what is happening in the dream. There is a beautiful extract from the Course that tells us: *"The holiest of all the spots on earth is where an ancient hatred has become a present love"*. T-26.IX.6: 1. Circumstances like having a sick body, losing a job or being broke are simply projected scenes that have no intrinsic meaning and as such can have no effect whatsoever on the state of peace in which the mind rests. And this is what we truly want, the peace that surpasses all understanding.

Does that mean that if a body is sick its destiny is to be sick, or that a situation will never change despite a change of mind? Not necessarily. If the mind, where the unconscious guilt resides, experiences healing, a side effect of the healing could be reflected in a change taking place in the form. A body could heal, a situation could change, etc. But what I want to emphasize is that whatever happens in the world of form is completely irrelevant. Once the mind is consciously aware that it is dreaming a dream, the content of the dream does not affects the mind, resulting in unbroken peace. As *A Course in*

Miracles says: *"The miracle establishes you dream a dream, and that its content is not true."* T-28.II.7:1

6 Example of everyday life to illustrate how true forgiveness would be implemented.

Let's start by remembering that the only problem we all experience is the same one; we believe that this dream is our reality. Identifying with a separate "I", with an "I" that has a body that is known as my identity, causes all the apparent problems we perceive. Hence *A Course in Miracles* reminds us: "He need not be forgiven but awakened." T-17.I.1: 3.

Let us also take into consideration that if awakening from a dream is the solution to every problem, then there must be a reason why we do not wake up. We've already said that it is unconscious guilt. But looking at it from a perspective that we can identify with: if I am aware that I am dreaming a dream, awakening would not be a problem. However, if I am not aware that I am dreaming a dream and instead believe I am the image that is being dreamed, awakening from the dream would be the equivalent of "dying". This is the fear feeding all earthly experience. So, let's begin by looking at what we call the practice of forgiveness using an example of a human experience. Pay close attention to what I am going to say. It may appear as if, in using an example that has to do with the human experience, the mind is kept distracted from Truth. In actuality it is a process by which the mind is trained where not to put its attention, so that the mind's attention can be redirected to where the only problem lies; in the mind and not in the form, not in the world.

Let's say I have money issues. The thought "there is not enough money" arises from my experience. I watch how I feel. The feeling has nothing to do with the thought "I do not have money". It has to do with the mind's interpretation of that thought. The interpretation could be, "that's bad", or "this should not be happening to me", or "if I had money I could have sustenance, I could support my family", "I feel so guilty for not being able to make money" etc. The mind can come up with millions of stories about what not having money means. For instance if I believe that money is needed in order for me to "live" then I have made money my sustenance and if, as a body, I have no sustenance I will surely "die." Observe that in reality the only problem is that I believe I am a body. By holding onto this belief, look at how astutely fear keeps the mind's attention in the dream by using the money issue as justification.

Let's take a look at the other side of the same coin. The thought "I have money" arises. And I believe it because when I look at my bank account there is plenty of money. I watch how I feel. I feel "good". This feeling has nothing to do with having money. It has to do with the mind's interpretation of the thought: "I have money". The mind fabricates stories about this thought starting with "that's good", or "I am someone valuable", or "I am happy because I have money", or "I am a better person", or "I can buy things for myself and for others", or "I have sustenance" and, just like the opposite (negative) thoughts about not having enough money, all of the new "positive" thoughts are the ego's strategies to hold on to the belief "I am a body" (pain and pleasure, as previously discussed). The underlying fear of dying (pain) remains, only this time it is covered up with the excuse, "I have enough to 'live'" (pleasure). Again, both are versions that serve the same purpose; to hold on to the belief that this physical experience is my "reality", albeit that in the second example we would not want to wake up from the dream. Why would I want to wake up from a dream that I am "enjoying?" Yet with or without money, it is still a dream of death, a dream that denies our True Essence which is eternal life!

So how is true forgiveness put into practice in this example? Simple:

1: I am aware that this world is not my reality, meaning I am also part of this illusion.

2: When the thought or emotion about money arises, I remember that they are just thoughts and emotions that mean nothing.

What Happened After Letting God

As *A Course in Miracles* reminds us: *"Nothing I see (nothing I perceive; thoughts, feelings, sensations, circumstances, etc.) means anything"*. W-pI.1. That's how the mind is released of content so the suffering and all the heaviness are taken away.

3: The peace that I feel when the mind is free of stories is the correction that corroborates that choosing the Holy Spirit's thought system is the only sane choice. Now I simply trust the process.

All I am doing with the practice of true forgiveness is: observing the stories that say the world is the cause of my "lack of peace" or of my "well-being"; and becoming aware of the feelings, whose sole purpose is to maintain the belief in the mind that I am a separate body, arise with them.

they mean nothing ie don't tell a story

I could use relationships issues, health issues, work issues, government issues and many more as examples. However, do you now think that a physical illness, a government issue, a loss of a family member, a loss of work, or its opposite, finding a relationships that makes you "happy", getting a good job, changes in government policy, etc., are "different" problems than the example I shared about money? And do you think that forgiveness would be applied in a "different" way to those "problems?" The answer would be no. It's all the same!

That is why *A Course in Miracles* reminds us: *"It is not difficult to understand the reasons why you do not ask the Holy Spirit to solve all problems for you. He has not greater difficulty in resolving some than others. Every problem is the same to Him, because each one is solved in just the same respect and through the same approach* (when there is a change of mentality as a result of true forgiveness). *The issues that need to be resolved do not change, regardless of the form the problem seems to take* (relationships, money, health, government, desire to be loved, etc.). *A problem can appear in many forms, and it will do so while the problem lasts* (the problem is that the mind's identification is with a separate body). *It serves no purpose to attempt to solve it in a special form. It will recur and then recur again and yet again, until it has been answered for all time and will not rise again in any form* (the mind has awakened). *And only then are you released from it"*. T-26.II.1: 1-8.

7 Why is it that I do not experience results when putting true forgiveness into practice?

When we put forgiveness into practice we always experience a result, inner peace. This peace is experienced even when perhaps the body continues to feel pain. Physical pain is an experience, while psychological pain is an interpretation, and the Holy Spirit works at the psychological level. He reinterprets what the ego mind has interpreted. This is known as the peace that surpasses all understanding. We must always be aware that forgiveness is not about "fixing" our problems in the world, but rather remembering that we are the dreaming mind, not the character that is being dreamed. All fear is derived from the belief that I am this separate body, while our Reality goes beyond this experience. As a result of true forgiveness we are gradually becoming aware of the fact that we are mind and not body. It is this that restores the peace.

Now, since the dreaming mind is the cause, a change of mind can lead to a change in the world of forms, in the sense that when our perception changes it is as if the world changes, even when nothing in the physical realm has changed. For example, let's say that someone has lost their job and that, consequently, the person feels "bad". We already know the reason for feeling bad has to do with personal interpretation about the experience. However, when there is a change of mentality as a result of choosing the Holy Spirit's thought system, the person might still be out of work but suffering ceases and the situation is perceived from a state of peace and equanimity. That is why *A Course in Miracles* is not interested in what happens in the dream, but rather in what happens in the mind. Then, from that space of clarity, the character in the dream may be directed to do and/ or to say something when necessary, or the circumstance could change without the character having to do or say anything. In that sense synchronistic or unexplainable events, often referred to as "miraculous" might take place. After all a dream is not governed by the laws of the dream, but by the laws of the mind that dreams the dream. But prior to any change in the dream, as a result of true forgiveness, peace has been restored in the mind and that is the only thing that matters. That's why I said that forgiveness always delivers the immediate result of peace of mind, regardless of circumstances.

8 What then is the purpose of forgiveness if it will not change anything in my dream?
The purpose of forgiveness at the level of form, at the level of this physical experience, is the end of suffering. It is the peace that surpasses all understanding by making me aware that I am the Whole and not a fragment of the Whole. When peace is established in the mind, what more would one want? At the level of the mind, it is to make it aware that it is mind and not body, and thus be able to awaken from this dream, but that is not something to concern ourselves with now. Let us use forgiveness for practical purposes, for what can be experienced here, the experience of inner peace. It can be called the experience of a happy dream.

9 How was it that the mind decided to dream this dream of separation?
Answering this question would simply affirm the belief that there was a separation. The Course addresses it as follows: "The ego will demand many answers that this Course does not give. It does not recognize as questions the mere form of a question to which an answer is impossible. The ego may ask, "How did the impossible occur?", "To what did the impossible happen?", and may ask this in many forms. Yet there is no answer; only an experience. Seek only this, and do not let theology delay you". C-In.4: 1-5.

So the question will only keep the mind focused on the dream, running around in circles. It is better to put all speculation to one side and concentrate on practicing forgiveness each time our peace is disturbed. Then, while we perceive ourselves as a body in this world, at least we will live in peace, free from suffering.

10 Is there anything wrong with asking for something you want?

First of all, it is necessary to always keep in mind that our reality is that we are mind and not separate bodies. This whole book, as well as *A Course in Miracles*, emphasizes again and again that our reality is God (Mind), not "human beings" (separate entities). Observe how the questions asked keep the emphasis on this "I" that is perceived as separate from the Whole (God, Mind), and that now wants things from the world (dream). This only reinforces the unconscious guilt in the mind, the belief that there was a separation. Since we are talking about two levels simultaneously, the question must be addressed from two perspectives: firstly at the level where we think we are, believing that we are this body that wants things so that we can become conscious of the consequences of that desire; and secondly by bringing the attention to the mind, to the goal of *A Course in Miracles* which is to undo the belief in separation.

It is not that there is anything "wrong" with wanting things in the world. We just want to be consciously aware of what is really going on. For a person who is not conscious of this awakening journey, wanting things is a process that occurs naturally since the one who desires is the one who feels separated, therefore experiences scarcity, lack. In that sense, part of the plan for his salvation would be to desire things, and in most cases, to obtain them. This is how one realizes, not from theory or speculation, but from direct experience, that the happiness and peace that is so much desired is not experienced as a result of obtaining anything from the world.

What we can do with these desires is to observe them and to bring awareness. If a desire persists, suppressing it or resisting it is not going to help. We can move in the direction of our desires with the awareness that they are not the source of our happiness. If the desire is fulfilled, that's fine. If the desire is not fulfilled, that is fine also. All expectation, all attachment to results are put aside because in fact attachment or expectation is the reason that suffering is experienced. In this sense, any desire becomes our curriculum for forgiveness. Then, without any sense of loss or sacrifice, that which was previously desired falls away because it ceases to have value.

There is an excerpt from an addendum to *A Course in Miracles* titled '*The Song of Prayer*' which explains: "*It is not easy to realize that prayers for things, for status, for human love, for external "gifts" of any kind, are always made to set up jailers and to hide from guilt. These things are used for goals that substitute for God, and therefore distort the purpose of prayer. The desire for them is the prayer. One need not ask explicitly. The goal of God is lost in the quest for lesser goals of any kind, and prayer becomes requests for enemies. The power of prayer can be quite clearly recognized even in this. No one who wants an enemy will fail to find one. But just as surely will he lose the only true goal that is given him. Think of the cost, and understand it well. All other goals are at the cost of God*". S-1.III.6:1-10.

Stepping on the scale is a prayer

The issue then is not whether there is something wrong with wanting anything from the dream world, but rather, is the dream world (the experience of feeling separate and scarce) what I really want? To use a more accessible word, is inner peace what I truly desire? For those who are still hanging on to their identity, what I have shared could generate an unsettling feeling, a sense of fear, the reason for which is obvious. If we have spent our entire life pursuing goals, dreams and experiences in the world that we thought would bring us happiness or would bring us peace, and that belief is strongly reinforced by the culture, by social media, the educational system, what can we do? ¡Forgive!

Just hold on firmly to the Hand of the Holy Spirit in a state of complete surrender and acceptance of what-is. Simply know that while the process of undoing fear is taking place, you will not remain helpless. As the mind´s perception changes through the practice of true forgiveness, all that was previously valued in the world is replaced with a true desire for inner peace, without any sense of loss or sacrifice. The experience of inner peace is like living in Heaven while experiencing ourselves on earth.

11 Where do desires come from?

According to *A Course in Miracles*, a desire comes from the mind that projects the body, not from the body. A desire could be described as unconscious guilt projected onto an object to reinforce the belief that there is an "I" "separate" from that which is "desired". I put these words in quotations because as we have already established, our Reality, being non-dual, holds no "I", no "separation", no such thing as "desire" since there is no "dream". Before continuing, observe how subtly this claim tries to have the mind scrambling for an answer that corroborates the belief that there is a separate being who can desire something. In reality, all desires derive from the original desire that "supposedly" gave rise to the apparent separation. These include the desire to feel special, the desire to feel separated from God by fabricating "my own world".

Yet in the same way that the "I" character appears to emerge out of nothing (is "born") and dissolves into nothing ("dies"), desires, thoughts, feelings that the character "I" appears to experience also emerge from nothing and dissolve into the nothing. This means that nothing need be done except to observe them and allow them to continue their course, in the same way that we observe our "human" experience unfolding without doing anything in particular about it.

All that needs to be done is to constantly bring awareness to the desires that will continue to arise as long as the mind holds on to its identity as a body, as a separate "I". This is done without feeling any guilt, without oppressing or ignoring any desire, recognizing that any desire towards an object or a worldly experience only serves to keep the mind distracted from true inner peace. They present only further opportunities to practice true forgiveness. *A Course in Miracles* reminds us: "*The Holy Spirit asks only this little help of you: Whenever your thoughts wander to a special relationship* (desire towards something in the world) *which still attracts you, enter with Him into a holy instant*

What Happened After Letting God   63 (*present moment without personal interpretations*), *and there let Him release you*". T-16.VI.12:1

12 I feel a great passion for what I do, do I still have to practice forgiveness?
The purpose of forgiveness is to undo the unconscious guilt in the mind. This makes what is done in the world of form (physical experience, in the dream) completely irrelevant. The fact that you feel passion for something in the world could be an indication that you are still giving value to the world and so the desire to awaken from the dream may not be appealing to you. Remember that to let go of something, you have to stop giving it value.

If you are already aware of this path, having recognized a deep call to remember Who You Are, but there is still a desire for the world, as long as you put that passion at the service of Truth, then enjoy it. The only difference is, if the time comes to let go of that which you feel so passionate about (let go of the dream), you will do so with a sense of inner peace and not the slightest feeling of any loss or sacrifice. In other words do not fight the passion for that would put you in conflict with yourself. Simply observe it and, if you are supposed to pursue it, this will happen in the same way that, if you are not supposed to do anything with it, that will happen too because the character in the dream is not in charge of its actions.

A simpler way in my experience to handle this passion issue would be to become the witness to the character "I" who is doing the things he likes, without making a big deal of it. This helps the mind identify itself with the consciousness that is aware of the experience instead of with the apparent "separate I" that appears to be having the experience. Using myself as an example, am I this "I" writing these words or is awareness aware of the "I" character through which words appear to be being written? As you can see, I am not ceasing to live life as it unfolds. It's just that worldly desires and worldly passions have been replaced by a desire for inner peace. Regardless of

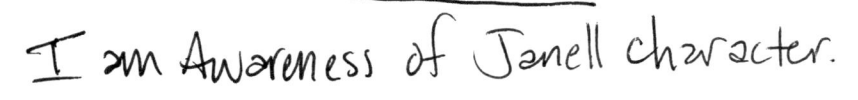

I am Awareness of Janell character.

the reason why, in my case, these words are being written: call them desire, passion, inspiration, as well as any passion that may be arising in you, the important thing is that *A Course in Miracles* is constantly reminding the mind that it is dreaming this dream, and that its Reality is God, Mind, Love, not this experience of "separation".

13 If a person or situation causes me pain and I practice forgiveness, am I supposed to feel something after doing the process?
The first thing to be aware of is that nothing "external" to us has the power to cause us pain or pleasure, for two reasons: one, there is nothing "external" to us; and two, the pain and pleasure that we feel is an interpretation we make about the "external". What the projection does is to grab the pain or pleasure that is already in me and project it onto an "external" image to justify it. It is a dead-end street. Approaching this question from our current level of experience, pain, like pleasure, immediately brings the mind's attention to the dream, verifying once again the belief that I am a body and not a mind. Therefore, the world is cause and I am its effect. But again, the opposite is true. The mind is the only cause (the one that projects the dream, which includes this "I") and the world, this "I" is the effect (projection).

True forgiveness, then, is put into practice so that "we" can become consciously aware that our identity is the mind dreaming the dream and not the character "I" within the dream. As a result, the experience I have is inner peace by immediately recognizing that what I feel is not caused by what I perceive, but again, by my interpretation of what I perceive. Or I should say, for what is perceived by the mind. That is what I refer to as being conscious. It is the end of all suffering. However, and this is extremely important, although it can't be denied that forgiveness offers an immediate sense of release from guilt, resulting in an experience of inner peace that could take the form of a challenging issue being resolved, the intention behind forgiveness must be understood. If I practice forgiveness so that I can feel a particular way, let's say, to stop feeling pain and feel more pleasure, or to seek resolution for a particular issue, I remain identified with this "I" and so the mind is still distracted from Truth, from inner peace.

The benefit of becoming consciously aware that causal power can no longer be attributed to the world, that nothing and no-one can affect my emotional state, is that forgiveness serves as a tool for making corrections in the mind (the one that is dreaming this dream, including "me"), the only place where true healing can occur. One can simply step back and watch the whole movie unfold with a sense of ease, without judging anything as either good or bad, and that is real peace, that is liberation, that is understanding.

14 I feel like I'm struggling with my financial situation and I do not understand how remaining in peace can help me.
Let's start where the problem lies, in the mind. Resisting any situation, in this case a financial situation, continues reinforcing the mind's belief in this "I", leading you up being a dead-end street. There is also the problem of the intrinsic error in the question, namely that our peace is derived from what happens in the world, from what takes place in the dream. Repeating the fundamental message of this book, peace can only be experienced when we become consciously aware that we are the dreamer of the dream, not the character "I" that appears to be living in the dream.

Once we make ourselves at least consciously aware of our true identity, the first thing to avoid in any situation is to "try to be at peace". Rather, surrender completely to the present moment leaving aside all personal interpretations. The term *A Course in Miracles* uses is the "Holy Instant." (T-15). This is how the Holy Spirit can heal the unconscious guilt and the mind is restored to its natural state of peace.

Looking at this experience called "financial situation issue" from a different perspective, it could be a great opportunity to bring to the surface unconscious beliefs that can now be looked at and undone. Let's say the person has financial problems because he is afraid to look for work, or he feels a lot of pride, so would be unwilling to do certain jobs, or whatever. The teaching here is not to be aware that he is not a body, but to observe how he is empowering some illusions over others, without realizing that if everything is a dream, there is really no difference between cleaning streets and being the president of a corporation. The practical thing would be to look honestly at all the unconscious or conscious beliefs that arise that do not allow for a functional adaptation in this world, while simultaneously practicing forgiveness in order to be aware that his reality is mind and not body. At least he would be at peace, whether is cleaning streets or handling the responsibilities of being a corporate president. From that space of inner peace, the character "I" will be directed to do whatever needs to be done, or not done, according to God's plan for the salvation of the mind.

15 How can I differentiate between the ego and the Holy Spirit when I make a decision?

You do not have the "free will" to make decisions. A dreamed character has neither personal will nor power to choose. You can only watch the script unfold and look at it with the Holy Spirit's thought system, thereby experiencing peace, or look at it with the ego's thought system, thereby experiencing suffering. But assuming that one could choose, the direct and practical answer would be: when there is no fear you know that whatever the decision, you are most likely following the Holy Spirit's suggestion. The Course puts it this way: *"Before you choose to do anything, ask me if your choice is in accord with mine. If you are sure that it is, there will be no fear"*. T-2.VI.4: 9-10.

Using my experience as an example, my power to make decisions, or my "free will", so to speak, has to do with the choice that is made in the mind. That choice is always the same, between the peace I desire (Holy Spirit) or my personal interpretations (ego). By leaving all interpretations aside (forgiving) (and I don't mean practical interpretations, I mean stories that the mind fabricates about a future or past that brings up worry and guilt), I simply trust whatever decision this body-mind organism called Nick [called Janell] feels inclined to make. From then on, I accept the new experience as my new curriculum for healing the mind, for practicing forgiveness.

16 If I feel a strong attraction towards someone, is that my ego?
Attraction could be said to be the sensation of lack that one experiences when perceiving oneself as separated. This lack is now projected onto a person or an object so that one can feel "complete". Since the question has to do with attraction towards a person, it is the ego at play. Remember that the ego is the belief in separation and attraction is the desire for union. The funny thing is, being the one mind, there is nothing to "join." Forgiveness brings us to this recognition.

Feeling attracted to someone or something implies that the dream still has value and I still take myself to be a body. Even knowing this, we are not asked to suppress the attraction, which is in fact impossible. That's why A Course tells us: "*I have said repeatedly that the Holy Spirit would not deprive you of your special relationships, but would transform them*". T-17.IV.2:3. We are merely asked to be aware that this attraction comes from the unconscious guilt that is generated in the mind and is not caused by any "external" experience. Let us invite a New Teacher (Inner Wisdom, Holy Spirit) which is the practice of true forgiveness, so that correction in the mind can take place and peace be restored in it.

Always remember that the only thing we have to do with everything we are attracted to is to change its purpose. In this way, instead of serving as a distraction, it can serve to bring the mind back to Truth.

17 What does it mean to change the purpose of a relationship?
Consciously or unconsciously, whenever we look for a relationship of any kind, whether at work or with friends or lovers, we do so with a predetermined purpose: to bring us happiness. What other reason would there be to enter into any kind of relationship? But that is not what matters. The

important thing is to be aware that if I want a relationship to make me happy, or to derive pleasure from it , I will end up suffering. *A Course in Miracles* reminds me: "*Anything in this world that you believe is good and valuable and worth striving for can hurt you, and will do so*". T-26.VI.1: 1. This is because in this dream everything changes. But the question now is, who is the "me" who wants a relationship in order to be happy? We must be constantly aware of how subtle this work is so that at least we don´t confuse the levels (dream and mind), for this is how the mind keeps distracting itself and makes the dream real. But since we perceive ourselves as bodies, in a world that seems very "real" to us, we begin from where we appear to be.

As an example of a romantic relationship, an analogy that I use in my talks is: imagine you are sleeping and you dream that you are on a beautiful beach in Fiji with the woman or man of your dreams. Would you like to wake up from such a dream? Generally, the answer would be no. If the purpose is to continue deriving pleasure from that image of Fiji in the mind, you would not want to wake up. However, what you do not know is that the pleasurable scene, being part of a dream that constantly changes, will change too, with the possibility of becoming a nightmare. Maybe this person you want so much dies (an inevitability inside the dream unless you are the one who dies first). The person may change his or her mind, or it may be you, who changes your mind about him or her. You could be betrayed or hurt. The body could become sick and the dying process could be prolonged for many years, and countless other events and scenarios might take place. If, on the other hand, you simply wake up from that dream, all possible scenarios will disappear instantly.

When you change the purpose of your relationships from making you happy to becoming conscious, all these potential scenarios are now put at the service of love and thus the Holy Spirit can free the mind of all fear. This is how the Holy Son of God (who we all are) happily wakes up from the dream, while enjoying whatever experiences may be taking place in the dream

What Happened After Letting God

because there is no attachment. *A Course in Miracles* states it this way: *"I said before that the first change, before dreams disappear, is that your dreams of fear are changed to happy dreams. That is what the Holy Spirit does in the special relationship. He does not destroy it, nor snatch it away from you. But He does use it differently, as a help to make His purpose real to you. The special relationship will remain, not as a source of pain and guilt, but as a source of joy and freedom"*. T-18.II.6: 3-7

18 How is a special relationship different from a holy relationship?

Given the fact that there is only one mind dreaming a dream, the only relationship that "exists" takes place in the mind, and it is between the mind relating to the ego's thought system (special relationship) or the mind relating to the Holy Spirit's thought system (Holy relationship).

If the mind is identified with the ego's thought system, the character "I" will relate to the world (dream) from a place of specialness. What that means is, believing myself to be a separate entity, living in a world of separation which I consider my "reality", I will spend my whole life avoiding pain and seeking pleasure. Feeling empty and lacking, I will continue chasing things in the world that I believe will make me happy or will bring me peace. I will react to circumstances and experiences, I will feel the desire to attack or will experience attack as a result of feeling like a victim or whatever story the ego's thought system adheres to in the mind. An underlying sense of fear will prevail, which I will attempt to avoid by finding ways to distract and entertain myself. All this stems from the ego's thought system which believes that I am a "body", a "person", a "separate entity".

On the other hand, when the mind identifies with the Holy Spirit thought system, the character "I" will relate to the world (dream) from a place of holiness. This means that since I am now consciously aware that I am the dreamer of the dream (not me the character but the mind that is dreaming me), I will not find myself reacting to any experiences in the dream. Feeling whole and complete, the need to chase things in the world stops. The character "I" may appear to have preferences, and in some cases will pursue those preferences, but without any attachment to them because his happiness and sense of peace does not depend on the attainment of any of his preferences. An underlying sense of peace will prevail throughout his life, regardless of the kinds of experiences taking place according to the script. As we can see, it has nothing to do with having a special or a Holy relationship with "another" because there are no "others".

Great explanation of H.S. identification

The typical confusion of levels is when I believe I am a person who is relating to another person and that the relationship between the "two" is either special or Holy. Once again, the relationship between the two does not exist because all that is taking place is the one mind (consciousness) projecting images. So every time you find yourself reacting to your circumstances, observe that what is really happening is that you have a strong identification with yourself as a separate entity. But while the reaction is taking place, if the mind complete surrenders to what is, a shift in awareness can take place. To use pain as an example, instead of saying "I am experiencing pain" we change it to "pain is being experienced". This is how the mind slowly stops identifying itself with a body and begins to identify with that (mind, consciousness), which is aware of a body.

19 What happens if my partner is not spiritual like me: should I stay with her or him?

From a non-dual perspective, "spiritual" is what belongs to the realm of Truth (uppercase). This physical experience is not spiritual, but rather a projection of separation, a dream. This being the case, no other thing or person in this world is "spiritual". The question has to do with compatibility, and that would simply bring forgiveness opportunities.

Having clarified this, every relationship happens, not by a personal decision, but by a meeting orchestrated by the mind

What Happened After Letting God

itself, containing all the perfect opportunities for forgiveness. Let me be clear that when I speak of a relationship I speak of any type of encounter. Only for the purposes of this question are we going to limit it to a romantic relationship. The Manual for the Teachers of *A Course in Miracles* reminds me: *"There are no accidents in salvation. Those who are to meet will meet, because together they have the potential for a holy relationship. They are ready for each other".* M-3-1: 6-8. If we are clear that the purpose of the relationship is to remember Truth, the relationship will last as long as necessary to serve that purpose. It may be for life or it may be temporary. If the purpose of the relationship is simply to derive pleasure from it, then it would be a matter of seeing how well two people get along, according to the script that is already written.

The important thing is that one continues to focus on the inner work, since salvation is for oneself, without the need to manipulate each relationship. As long as the relationship is put at the service of Truth, the Holy Spirit will know what to do with it. If the relationship ceases to serve its purpose, it will dissolve by itself, and there will be nothing anyone can do to prevent this from happening. What will be avoided when a relationship's purpose changes from deriving pleasure from it to remembering Truth will be the suffering.

There is, then, no answer to this question regarding what to do or what not to do, because you are not even choosing anything anyway. The question is, rather, what purpose will be assigned to the relationship?

20 How can I deal with people who bother me, who press my buttons, who do not respect my space, etc.?
Being already aware that the world is an effect of the mind and not something that is happening to me, all these experiences are perceived as great opportunities to look at the content of my mind so that I can put into practice true forgiveness. As fear is being undone, the character "I" that I take myself to be is in a better position to handle any experience that comes along.

The difference is that whatever decision is made comes from a place of understanding so it will be the most appropriate and it will be devoid of guilt. In short, without blaming or justifying your feelings, if someone bothers you, maybe the most loving thing would be to leave, or to tell them how you feel without projecting your anger. You can set limits, if that is what the situation requires as long as you remember that, *"I am not a victim of the world I see"*. W-pI.31.I. Now it's a matter of using each experience as the curriculum for practicing true forgiveness.

21 How can I discipline my children and do it peacefully when in reality what I feel is frustration and anger when they behave in a certain way?

We do not really discipline anyone even if it seems to be the case. Everything we do in the world is an effect of the thought system with which the mind is identified in each moment. If the mind is identified with the ego's thought system, the discipline will come loaded with guilt, anger, impatience. If the mind is identified with the Holy Spirit's thought system, the same action, if necessary, will be inspired by love. What happens is that we believe that if the children behave in a certain way we can be happy. Another way of saying it: we have made our children a "god" to whom we have assigned the power to determine our state of mind. That is what we have done with the world. But the lesson of forgiveness is always the same, no matter the scenario.

As with all experience that seems to be the "cause" of some type of feeling in us, we recognize that this feeling is not caused by something "external", in this case the behavior of the children. Whatever we feel is what is repressed in the unconscious and this, in turn, is projected onto "external" images (behavior of the children) in order to justify the desire to feel like a victim. The awareness of this helps us return the attention to the mind. This is where we open ourselves to a change of mentality that comes from the Inner Wisdom (Holy Spirit).

What Happened After Letting God

There are two small books that I highly recommend on how to approach the parent-child relationship written by Dr. Kenneth Wapnick, based on the teachings of *A Course in Miracles*. These are: *'Parents and Children: Our Most Difficult Classroom'* Part One and Part Two.

22 *How is it possible that at times I could manifest things easily and now I feel I cannot manifest anything?*
The fundamental error is to believe that there is an "autonomous self" that "manifests" things in the world. The only "manifestation", and even then it is not real, is the apparent manifestation of an "I" in a "world". Just like in a dream, the figures that are being dreamt cannot make decisions or manifest anything. They are simply projections of a mind that dreams a dream. Given this, the "who" that apparently "manifest" things, is the mind itself.

For the purpose of addressing the question, and assuming that there is a separate "I" that "manifests," God's plan for salvation is for the mind to be aware that it is a dreaming mind. For this to happen, it must first begin to question its identity as a separate, limited individual at the mercy of the laws of the world he made. This starting point of believing I am a body, a separate individual learning about the power of the mind, or should I say the power to "manifest", serves as an opening for the mind to begin questioning its notion of reality.

As the mind becomes more conscious that who I am is not this body, somehow the ego's thought system takes this understanding and starts using it to its advantage by dabbling with the "power of the mind". I can see, for example, that sometimes I have "manifested" what I desired, overlooking the fact that over 90 % of the time I have been unable to manifest what I wanted.

The reason is if I could manifest everything I wanted there would be no motivation for me (the mind) to awaken from the dream. One could ask, but why can I not manifest what I want and have a wonderful dream? This is because within the dream that is by its nature dual, it is impossible to experience the "good" without its opposite. In Truth our True Nature, all that there is, Oneness, Love has no opposites. The mind is attempting to regain this experience which is why, sooner or later, we find ourselves seeking. We are seeking eternal peace, we are seeking true happiness. Once I am consciously aware that the power to manifest no longer works (and actually it never did, it was just part of the script) or I think I have "manifested" what I thought I wanted and still I'm not at peace, the mind begins to shift from wanting to manifest anything to desiring peace of mind. So everything, including the "manifesting" part, is a part of God's plan for salvation.

23 While I practice forgiveness and I let go, how can I manage my life?
As you have always done, only in peace due to the practice of forgiveness. There is an excerpt from the Course that says: *"There is a way of living in the world that is not here, although it seems to be. You do not change appearance, though you smile more frequently. Your forehead is serene; your eyes are quiet"*. W-pI.155.1: 1-3.

Remember that it is not the "I" character that "manages" his life. Life manages itself. That is why there is nothing that "I" have to "do" except leave aside my personal interpretations (judgments) and learn to forgive. What the character "I" does or does not do in the world is an effect that simply reflects the thought system with which the mind is identified in each moment. If the mind chooses fear (ego's thought system), the choices that the character "I" seems to make will reflect that choice in the mind. If the thought system of the Holy Spirit is chosen in the mind, the behavior of the character "I" will reflect that choice. It's that simple.

24 If everything goes well in my life, I love what I do, I enjoy the money I make, I love things as they are, is there anything wrong with experiencing that life?
It is not that there is something intrinsically "wrong". It is that

What Happened After Letting God

as long as the mind continues to value the world, there will be no desire to awaken from the dream. But as the ego's mantra is *"Seek and do not find"* T-12.IV.1: 4, behind every pleasure there is pain. And if you think you are "happy" because things go one way or another, believe it or not, the happiness you experience is not true happiness because it is being conditioned by your experiences. When you become aware of your True Nature as peace, that you are mind and not body, paradoxically you enjoy all your experiences without labeling some as "better" than others. This means that if things go one way, fine. If things go a different way, that´s fine too. This attitude is known as the peace that surpasses all understanding.

But do not make the mistake of believing that because things go one way or another it means that you are being aware of Truth. Truth transcends this physical experience. What happens in the dream is part of the dream and what happens in Truth is part of Truth. That is why we are told: *"Render to Caesar the things that are Caesar's; and to God the things that are God's"* [Matthew 22:21]. If the mind wants the dream with all its pleasures, the mind is choosing death. Because the fact is that this dream, however "pleasant" it may seem, ends in death. Conversely, when the mind chooses Truth, it chooses Eternal Life.

When awareness is brought to each present moment, you can fully enjoy each experience, free from guilt and free from attachment. In other words, you play with the toys without taking ownership of any, ready at all times to let them go when the call to return Home is heard.

25 Is there male and female energy?
Returning to the analogy of the dream, there is only one mind dreaming a dream and it is neither "feminine" nor "masculine", even though in the dream it seems to be masculine and feminine (differences). It is not energy either because energy, although it cannot be destroyed, can be transformed. And the transformation only happens between differences. *A Course in Miracles* states it this way: *"Whatever is true is eternal, and cannot*

change or be changed. Spirit is therefore unalterable because it is already perfect..." T-1.V.5: 1-2.

Not only do masculine and feminine "exist" in the dream but so too does up and down, inside and outside, light and dark, pain and pleasure, hot and cold, this and that. All these are polarities so cannot be a part of Truth since Truth is One: it is God, Love, or whatever you want to call it. Everything that has an opposite or can be changed such as "energy", "gender" etc., is illusory. In Truth, in what is One, neither male nor female can exist. There is only God.

26 I have been taught that prayer is an integral part of my spiritual development, but if everything is an illusion, what would be the purpose of prayer?
If the prayer is perceived as a request for something, a plea, then the mind is distracted from its state of unity, from its natural state of fulfillment. The focus remains on the "I" character that appears to be in the dream perceiving itself as separated from everything. The Song of Prayer, an addendum to *A Course in Miracles* states: *"To ask for the specific is much the same as to look on sin and then forgive it"*. C-1.I.4: 2. This only reinforces fear.

If true prayer is used as an opportunity to remember what I really am, this requires only silence and the willingness to leave aside any conditioned interpretation. Then each moment is a state of prayer. The Song of Prayer tells us: *"Prayer is a stepping aside; a letting go, a quiet time of listening and loving. It should not be confused with supplication of any kind, because it is a way of remembering your holiness"*. C-1.I.5: 1-2. Having said that, if it is necessary for you to pray for things, that being a part of your curriculum, your action is as correct as any experience that is taking place in this dream.

I strongly suggest you read *The Song of Prayer*, an addendum to *A Course in Miracles*. It is a very short book which goes into detail on the subject of prayer.

27 I have a partner that I love. I also have friends that I love.

Then there are people that I do not know, as well as people that I do not like. How then is it possible to love everyone in the same way?

The concept that we have of "love" based on separation has to do with the idea that "I love" that which makes me feel "good". Why do I "love" my partner, why do I "love" my family? Why do I "love" this or that? Because, believe it or not, I "love" them because of what I believe I derive from them. But what happens when they stop meeting my needs, or don't behave in a way that I like or want? They now become those people who I don't like, or who "make me" feel "bad". (I no longer "love" them) as I hold the belief that the world is cause and I experience its effect. None of this has to do with love. It is simply a game of manipulation sustained by the unconscious fear of feeling incomplete, of feeling separate. So in reality, what the world labels "love" is actually pleasure.

The Love (uppercase) we are talking about is the recognition of what I really am. When I recognize that I am the One Mind (Love), I cannot help but be aware that everything that I perceive as "separated" from me must be a part of me. Consequently, those people who I don't like, or I should say, whom I judge, simply allow me to see the obstacles to love that I have placed in me, that I conveniently project onto "them" so that I can justify my sense of victimhood and righteousness from the belief that I am a "separate" self.

Being consciously aware that the world is a mirror helps me to put forgiveness into practice so that the mind can be restored to its natural state of Love. The recognition of Universal Love in me now extends to everything. This is how I can love everyone and everything the same way, because there are no others! Meanwhile, in the physical form, the expression of affection will change between people. I will show affection in one way to my family, a different way to my romantic partner, a different way to a "stranger" and there may be people whom I would prefer not to spend time with, but what remains is the Love, meaning the Connection in which we are all a part.

28 I would like to be in a relationship. Should I go out into the world and do something so that this experience can take place?
At the level of the mind, where the physical experience is a dream, the purpose of the question is to keep the mind distracted from Truth. To want a partner is a "different" way of saying, I want the world. So the desire for a partner is no different than desiring a healthy body, a bank account full of money, a new car, travel to an exotic country, having a house on the beach, the government changing its policies, justice being done in this world etc., etc., etc.

Let's look at this question more closely from the character's apparent perspective. If I want a relationship, I can do what I feel inclined to do so that the desire can be fulfilled. The difference is, if the relationship takes place, and I place it in the service of Truth, then it is used to undo the unconscious guilt. If my desire is to derive pleasure, well-being and happiness from it, it will serve the ego's purpose which is to reinforce the belief in separation.

The important thing is to recognize the purpose behind the interpretation of your experiences, in this case, a relationship. Remember that the one who desires something, the one who needs something, is the "me" who feels lacking and separated. It is the one who is simply seeking fulfillment where it will never find it, namely in this world. But as you pay attention to what really matters, inner peace (forgiveness), the Holy Spirit will help you undo the unconscious guilt. The great benefit of being guilt-free is that you can enjoy the experience of a relationship if that is what comes your way, without fear of "losing" it - for there is no attachment.

29 Should I or should I not study with another teacher or attend another seminar?
In reality there is no "should" or "should not" because things are or are not. Either you are studying with a teacher or not. Either you are attending a seminar or not. All behavior is a reflection of our state of mind. If the mind is identified with

the ego's thought system (fear), it could be that I find myself looking for teachers and/or attending seminars that somehow feel they can satisfy my apparent personal need, diverting me from Truth. If the mind is identified with the Holy Spirit's thought system (Inner Wisdom), it can take the form of teachers and/or seminars that support the remembrance of Truth. As we can see, there are no rules. There is only the desire for Truth, or not. If the desire for Truth is there, every curriculum will be used for the fulfillment of that deep desire. If the desire for Truth is not there, interestingly enough, every curriculum will also serve the purpose of the awakening of consciousness. This is not because some of these paths point towards Truth, but because as the mind realizes that true peace of mind is not achieved through any of those paths, they will be abandoned. It's like a process of elimination where all roads lead to Rome. This reminds me of a Course lesson that says: *"God's plan for your salvation will work, and other plans will not"*. W-pI.71.8: 2.

30 What does it mean that there is no order of difficulty in miracles?

Could it not be inferred that a terminal illness requires a more complex miracle than a cold? And what could we say about war? Would not that be more difficult to solve than a simple discussion with a friend? Let us remember that the miracle takes place when the mind is aware of its nature as mind. This is what the Holy Spirit offers us when we choose His thought system; a change of mentality. Where fear was once perceived, love is now experienced.

When the mind becomes conscious of its true nature as mind, as the dreamer of the dream, nothing that takes place in the dream can affect its true nature as peace. That's why there is no order of difficulty in miracles, because no matter what happens in a dream, the miracle, being a change in perception, recognizes it is all a dream. It may be dreaming that the character in the dream has a terminal illness or that he is at war. It can also dream that the war has ended just as it can dream that the disease has been cured, and yet, these are not "miracles" but rather an exchange of illusions.

Always remember that forgiveness [Miracle:] is to heal the mind of the belief in separation, not to fix or change the dream. The darkness is not eradicated by trying to change it. It is eradicated by turning on the light. And again, a miracle is just the recognition that I am the dreamer of the dream, as the Course reminds me: *"The miracle does not awaken you, but merely shows you who the dreamer is"*. T-28.II.4:2

31 How do I know I'm ready for this awakening process?
Because you're going through it.

32 How can I prepare myself for the awakening process?
That is not up to you. That is decided by the mind that dreams you. So forget this question and simply appreciate that you are beginning to be aware, which is an indication that the mind is in its process of awakening.

33 How long will it take to wake up from this dream?
This is a misleading question because it assumes that this dream is real, and that at some point we will wake up. But the reality is that God never separated from Himself. You are advised to eradicate the question, "how long will it take to awaken", and focus instead on the forgiveness lessons that appear on a daily basis. Concerning yourself with how long it will take to awaken will not lead to the experience of awakening. It will instead keep the mind holding on the belief that there is an "I" who has to awaken. But the practice of forgiveness allows us to live in peace and happiness while we still perceive ourselves as characters in a dream of separation. This ought to be the only focus. Otherwise such questions will only serve to keep the mind distracted, speculating on an experience that can only take place when the mind itself ceases to exist.

34 When I see war and conflict in the world, how do I respond to it?
First I observe how I feel. If I am reacting to the scenario, I follow the practice of true forgiveness. I allow the Holy Spirit

to support me in being consciously aware that only love is real, which would lead to a change in perception that shows me that the separation never occurred. Once sanity is restored in the mind, what I feel directed to do will be an action inspired by love and not by fear. What was previously perceived as war and conflict is now recognized as a call for love.

It is always important to remember that what I appear to be seeing "outside" is simply a projection of the mind. Or as the Course would put it: "...*the outside picture of an inward condition*". T-21.In.1: 5. The inward condition is the belief in separation, which is projected as "different" scenarios (outside picture) starting from the premise that there is a "me" separate from the "world". Therefore, even a world filled with people doing "well" supports the mind´s belief in separation. As the mind heals, whatever scenario will start to have no effect on "me" until the mind is completely healed. And in that case the dream of separation is dissolved.

35 How is it possible that some people say they see a beautiful world while what I see is destruction?

Lesson 8 of *A Course in Miracles* reminds us: "*No one really sees anything. He sees only his thoughts projected outward*". W-pI.8.1: 2-3. One is not in the world seeing people saying that they see a beautiful world. The world is in the mind and it projects people, some saying that they see a precious world in the same way that an "I" is projected that believes that is seeing people saying they see a beautiful world. See the trap?

There is no ugly or precious world because: "*There is no world! This is the central thought the Course attempts to teach*". W-pI.132.6:2-3. Beautiful, good, destructive, bad are all labels that are attributed to neutral images that only serve to support the fundamental belief in the mind that says "I am a separate entity."

The same image can be perceived as pleasant or unpleasant. That is why *A Course in Miracles* works with the mind, at the attitudinal level. The change in mentality that the Course offers makes us aware that everything that the senses perceive is false. It does not go into games of "pretty" "ugly", "good" "bad", "nice" "unpleasant", etc. but only differentiates between what is True (Love, God) and what is false (fear, illusions).

36 How do I know if I am advancing on my spiritual path?
This question has to be discarded because it is a trap. In reality there is no "spiritual advance". There is only a dream that lacks content and nothing else. All we are doing with this work is observing how reality is given to the dream. Through the power of true forgiveness our minds are changed. The ego is the one that evaluates "spiritual advance" because that is how it can sustain its identity as a character that is now "advancing".

The question might be better asked as follows: How do I know that I am benefitting from this teaching? The answer would be when events, circumstances, or experiences that in the past had an effect on me, no longer have it. Another possible response would be when I see fear coming to the surface and I immediately apply forgiveness before the mind drifts. This does not imply that I am more or less advanced than anyone, since that would increase arrogance, but it does bear witness to the fact that I am becoming more conscious. For the purposes of the question, this is what could be considered as an advance.

37 I'm confused about the difference between creation and projection. If I'm projecting something, is it not the same as saying that I'm creating it?
When we speak of creation we are talking about Truth, about God. The mind in its natural state is creative. God is creative and the only thing He creates is more of Himself and so God does not "give" but extends. At the moment when the mind appears to divide itself, it perceives itself separated from itself. By perceiving itself as separated from itself, the mind projects a world that confirms the belief in separation.

What I am about to say is something abstract so I do not know the extent to which this analogy can serve as an accurate example. It is my attempt to use words to explain the inexplicable.

What Happened After Letting God

Returning to the dream analogy, let's say that when I am awake I am in my natural state of creation. In this state where there is only one, I recognize myself everywhere. Everything is part of me. I do not see differences, I only experience unity, like a newborn baby who can't perceive anything separate from himself or herself.

The moment the creative self gets into bed, closes its eyes and goes to sleep, a dream is projected in the mind, the only mind that there is, of that creative self. This dream is the projection that keeps that creative self, distracted from itself. The whole focus of the mind is on the dream, denying its identity as a mind, believing itself to be that tiny projected character interacting with other characters in a world within the dream. All this is part of the projection. Therefore I (capital letter) as Mind, God is in a constant state of creation while this "i" (lowercase letter), a character within the dream, not only experiences the projection, it is part of the projection.

38 What does cause and effect mean according to A Course in Miracles?

First we must clarify that in the world of dreams there is no cause and effect because the dream itself is an effect and, therefore, everything that takes place within the dream is an effect. The cause of which the Course speaks is the mind that projects the dream. *A Course in Miracles* says: *"This is a Course in cause and not effect".* T-21.VII.7: 8.

The ego, whose sole purpose is to keep the mind distracted within the dream, supports the belief that I am a separate, autonomous character, with the free will to make decisions and produce effects. For example, according to the ego's thought system, I (autonomous body) decide what I want. Then I start moving in the direction of getting what I want (cause). Finally, I experience the desired experience (effect). In the world of metaphysics the same example is used regarding the "power" of the mind. I think, feel or visualize what I want to manifest (cause), and if what I desire is manifested, that would be the effect.

The problem is that all that I think I am doing or visualizing "now" is part of a script that is already written, and was undone the moment the apparent "separation" took place. Remember, at the moment when the mind apparently "separated" itself, when it "fell asleep", when the thought of separation apparently "occurred", at that same moment, God woke the mind up. Only in that tiny moment was the concept of time introduced even though now it seems to last thousands of years. That is why this dream is a constant recreation of the same, even when the scenarios appear to be "different". The 'Manual for the Teachers of *A Course in Miracles* states it this way: *"The world of time is the world of illusion. What happened long ago seems to be happening now. Choices made long since appear to be open; yet to be made. What has been learned and understood and long ago passed by is looked upon as a new thought, a fresh idea, a different approach. Because your will is free you can accept what has already happened at any time you choose, and only then will you realize that it was always there. As the Course emphasizes, you are not free to choose the curriculum, or even the form in which you will learn it. You are free, however, to decide when you want to learn it. And as you accept it, it is already learned..."* M-2.3:1-8.

If the script is written, can "I" actually "choose" what I want? Here I ask you to please not believe anything I'm saying. Just do your own personal investigation. Ask yourself the question: Have I really been able to manifest everything I've wanted? In other words, have "I" been the "cause" of what has taken place in my experience? If you are honest with yourself you will realize that only on a few occasions does it appear that "it was you" that made the effects take place. In the vast majority of cases the reality has been that things have gone as they have, regardless of how much effort you have invested.

This understanding could generate the following question: Do I not sometimes create what I intended, what I visualized, what I decreed or manifested? Was that not the power of my desire, the power of my mind? After living for a few years the answer becomes very obvious. The ego has to succeed from time to time, otherwise you could not trust in it. I recognize that generally speaking you need to have lived long enough, have had enough experiences in the world, to realize that things happen according to a plan that is completely out of your control.

When the mind is open to this understanding, in practice, the projection of cause and effect can be employed in service of awakening. In other words, setting aside this idea that "I" (person) is the cause of anything, when "I" (person) find myself reacting to any projected image (effect), and what I refer to as image can be a feeling, a thought, a circumstance, it is simply an indication that I am experiencing myself as a separate body, therefore I am identified with the ego's thought system. This is all I have to remember to put into practice true forgiveness and thus identify with the Holy Spirit's thought system. Once that change of mentality takes place, the dream (world of effects) ceases to have an effect on me (dreaming mind, original cause). This is to return the attention to the true and only cause (mind). In the end, when peace of mind become the most important priority, knowing that nothing the world can offer can be the cause of it, the mind begins to rest in each present moment, and happiness is the eternal effect.

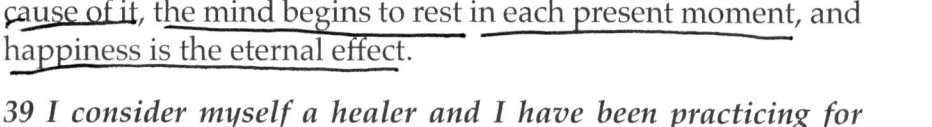

39 *I consider myself a healer and I have been practicing for many years. Now I am confused because if everything is an illusion, does that mean that I should stop doing the work I love so much?*
The problem here is the "healer" label. If I believe that I am "healing" someone, I am establishing a difference, a separation. This only supports the belief that I am a separate individual in a "real" dream "healing" "others." On top of that, believing that I am the "I" who heals, I cannot allow myself to be healed.

What is being healed is the mind´s belief that is a separate, individual entity apart from God. *A Course in Miracles* reminds us: *"Salvation is for the mind... This is the only thing that can be saved and the only way to save it"*. T-12.III.5: 1-2. In this sense the Holy Spirit is the only Savior, the only Healer. However, here in the world we pretend to exercise different roles. Since in this moment I am writing this book, I could easily use the label of writer, or author. If in your case the label of the healer applies to the work you are doing, knowing that there is "no one" to be "healed", that what is being healed is the mind's belief in separation, and that it is not "you" who does the "healing", simply do this: put yourself and your practice in the service of the Holy Spirit while continuing to play your role until life decides what to do with you next. If a change in career has to take place in your curriculum, it will.

40 If the body is an illusion, does that mean that I can eat what I want? And what about being a vegetarian or being aware of the foods I eat to keep my body healthy?
The body may be an illusion but our experience here says that it is not. Denying this only serves to perpetuate fear in the mind. As *A Course in Miracles* says: *"The body is merely part of your experience in the physical world. Its abilities can be and frequently are overevaluated. However, it is almost impossible to deny its existence in this world. Those who do so are engaging in a particularly unworthy form of denial"*. T-2.IV.3: 8-11.

Although we know theoretically that all this experience is illusory, what sustains it is unconscious guilt. As long as your experience is that of believing you are a body, you do what any person would do to stay "healthy". I put the word healthy in quotation marks because it is not diet or exercise that determines the "health" of the body, but rather the script that each particular body has to live.

The important thing is not to make a big deal out of anything that happens in this physical experience. Do what you feel inclined to do with your body, adhere to the diet that resonates with you, all the while knowing that whatever decision you seem to be making, it is not being made by "you". That is the

What Happened After Letting God

ultimate paradox.

41 How does the Course address reincarnation and, consequently, karma?

The 'Manual for the Teacher' of *A Course in Miracles* addresses the question of whether reincarnation exists as follows: *"In the ultimate sense, reincarnation is impossible. There is no past or future, and the idea of birth into a body has no meaning either once or many times. Reincarnation cannot, then, be true in any real sense. Our only question should be, "Is the concept helpful?"* M-24.1: 1-4.

The concept can be useful if we use it to be aware that we are not a body. If not it generates guilt or fear by implying that I am experiencing consequences in this "life" for what I did in a "past life", or I have to be careful with what I do in this "life" to avoid consequences in a "future life". Then the concept of reincarnation can be discarded. Remember that a dreaming mind does not "reincarnate". It is simply the only thing that exists. It can have multiple dreams, with different characters, and that is what, from the perspective of the dream, would give the appearance of reincarnation. But the dreaming mind, the eternal "I" never changes.

Karma, seen from the perspective of the Course, is instant cause and effect. This is the basis of the idea that what you give you receive. For example if I judge (condemn), I am instantly experiencing the effects of that judgment. That is my karma. If I love, I am instantly experiencing the effects of that love, and again, that is my karma. It has nothing to do with the past or the future. I heard someone say that the way I react to you is my karma. However, the way you react to me is yours.

42 What could be said about why babies are born with severe defects?

Questions like this overlook the fact that reality is God, not this world of separation. The world of illusions, the projected dream in which we pretend to live, is dual – everything that exists comprises opposites. If you want healthy babies, you will have to accept sick babies. There cannot be a part in this world without its counterpart. The objective of this physical experience is not to understand it but to transcend it. So the question of babies being born with severe defects would be replaced by asking ourselves what the experience can be used for. The answer is very simple: for practicing forgiveness.

43 It is said that God projected this world to be able to experience its opposite and thus have the experience it could not have in a state of unity. How does A Course in Miracles address this statement?
Speculations and statements about the origin of this world can be many. The objective of the Course is not to enter into debates or disagreements with any statement presented. Nevertheless the Course offers a version that, for me, is more in line with what a loving God would be. If we observe this world we see that it represents division, and the obvious scenes that we perceive could not be originated by an absolute love. According to the Course, God Is, and there is nothing else. This dream that appears to be taking place is a projection of a part of the mind that is perceived as separate from God. That part of the mind is known as ego. The ego is responsible for the projection. However, regardless of whether one believes that the projection came from God, or from whatever, the function of the Course is always the same: to return the mind to its natural state of unity and love and not allow it to be distracted by appearances.

44 How does A Course in Miracles address the issue of abundance, especially when it is said that service to others is the key to experiencing it?
First of all, we must recognize that this physical world, this dream represents separation with the result that everything experienced here is scarcity, lack. True abundance according to the teachings of *A Course in Miracles* is experienced when we recognize our true essence, our reality in God: "A sense of separation from God is the only lack you really need correct". T-1.VI.2: 1.

When you serve "others" for the purpose of experiencing

"abundance" you are reinforcing the belief in separation because the mind is establishing a difference - "you" and "others". Again, these "good intentions" solidify the unconscious guilt in the mind. Like the Course says: *"Trust not your good intentions, ..."* T-18.IV.2: 1.

Does this mean that I should not help a brother who asks for help? That is not what it means. It means simply that if I continue practicing forgiveness, offering all experience in the service of love, it will be another opportunity to become consciously aware of my True nature. I will remember not only what I really Am, but what my brother really Is: not a "body" that needs "help", but a part of the Whole, lacking nothing. Then I can even respect that his curriculum, while not appearing too pretty on the surface, is his path to awakening. And the help that I may end up offering, if that is what I am guided to do, won't be motivated by guilt, but inspired by love.

45 Are there people through whom God communicates?

For a non-dual theory to have any meaning, there cannot be more than one. A conversation is something that can only happen when there is more than one. That is the first thing to be aware of. Secondly, if God communicated with someone in the dream, that in itself would confirm the belief that there was a separation, which by the way, is the fundamental belief that holds the identity of an ego. So it could be inferred that God does not communicate with anyone in the dream.

However, there is a memory in the mind that constantly reminds the mind itself that its reality is God. Since the mind is so identified with the images that are part of the dream, the Holy Spirit uses those same images to facilitate awakening. The Holy Spirit (the Voice speaking for God) can take any form to remind the mind to stop paying attention to the dream. The Course says: "His ability to deal with symbols enables Him to work with the ego's beliefs in its own language". T-5.III.7: 2 If the communication takes place through a "spiritual teacher", that person does not make it anything special. He or she simply shares what has to be shared in the moment according to his or her role, one that he or she did not choose, and will teach through example.

46 If I love the ego can I heal it?

This question depends on what loving it means to you. If loving has to do with giving it reality and then loving it to "heal" it, this is a waste of effort. The ego cannot be healed because the ego does not exist. The ego is simply a belief in separation which in turn projects a dream to keep the mind distracted from Truth. All you have to do is return the attention to the mind, to the thought system of the Holy Spirit. This way, the ego weakens until there is no sense in holding on to it (to the belief in it). If loving it means not resisting it, not paying attention to it, not giving it power, then it is not that you are "loving" the ego, it is that you are not allowing yourself to be disturbed by it. Consequently, you become aware of the love that you are. It is not the ego that is being healed but the belief in it.

47 If meditation is a means of contacting my Self, is there any specific way to practice it? And if so, how much time should I devote to meditation, how regularly should I do it, and what kind of responses should I expect to receive?

Meditation is, I feel, a very useful tool when we begin our journey towards remembering Truth. As the mind is so confused, it serves to temporarily relax it and begin a process of conscious discernment. Only there is a small detail. I found after many years that meditation had become a mental activity whose purpose was to control my thoughts, or to lead me to experience some kind of "state of advanced consciousness" so to speak. I was not aware that all this activity served rather to keep the mind absorbed in perpetuating the belief that there is a "separate self" undertaking an activity called meditation. The ego's thought system uses spirituality, in this case the practice of meditation, not for the purpose of undoing itself, but for the purpose of forging a "spiritual" character within the dream.

Meditation for me has become the experience of living each

moment in complete acceptance of what is. I leave aside any personal interpretation and consciously observe the content of the mind. Any thoughts or sensations that arise are seen as nothing to do with me as consciousness. If I want to close my eyes and be silent, I'll do it, not as a mandatory routine but because I feel inclined to do so. I could say this is what consciousness is doing through this body-mind named Nick Arandes. It is what arises spontaneously. The 'Manual for the teacher' of *A Course in Miracles* reminds us: "*Routines as such are dangerous, because they easily become gods in their own right, threatening the very goals for which they were set up*". M-16.2: 5. This makes me aware of the consequences of using meditation or any practice that involves the sense of "I" doing something "important" or "special" within the dream. Firstly it perpetuates the belief that I am a separate self, attempting to attain whatever it is I think the meditation practice will give me. Secondly, and this is a result of holding on to the belief in the specialness of the practice, if for some reason I cannot do the practice one day and so I am not experiencing peace, this tool (meditation or spiritual practice) that "supposedly" was designed to help, has actually become an obstacle.

If meditation is employed to help the mind become aware that it is a dreaming mind and not this dreamed body, forgiveness and meditation are the same thing. If something happens and I do not react because I have withdrawn all meaning, I am meditating. As you can see, now the practice of meditation is not restricted to a specific time, to a specific place, nor to a specific physical position. It is what takes place at all times.

48 I feel confused about the subject of sex. It feels so good. However, is it another distraction from awakening?
Pleasure as well as pain are both experienced as a result of mind's identification with a body. As such they are a barrier to Truth. *A Course in Miracles* tells us: "*Sin shifts from pain to pleasure, and again to pain. For either witness is the same, and carries but one message:* "*You are here, within this body, and you can be hurt. You can have pleasure, too, but only at the cost of pain.*" These

witnesses are joined by many more. Each one seems different because it has a different name, and so it seems to answer to a different sound. Except for this, the witnesses of sin are all alike. Call pleasure pain, and it will hurt. Call pain a pleasure, and the pain behind the pleasure will be felt no more. Sin's witnesses but shift from name to name, as one steps forward and another back". T-27.VI.2: 1-9.

I cannot leave the answer there because when those desires that seem to be very "natural" for the "human being" arise, they could induce guilt. Everything that the body seems to feel comes from the mind that dreams it. So we do not want to be at war with our desires but to be aware that they are a part of a belief system based on the idea of separation. What can we do then to heal the mind so that these sexual impulses cease to be a distraction? We start with not judging them as good or bad. We allow them to manifest without suppressing them, without paying much attention to them. In other words, do not endow sex with the qualities of something "sacred" or "special".

Like sex, eating, sleeping and breathing are all part of a set of apparent needs that supports the underlying belief in the mind that says I am a body. As forgiveness continues to be put into practice in the service of a genuine desire for Truth, all the desires and impulses that appeared to be "physical", but which have always been originated in the mind, in due course vanish. Whatever happens will work towards the awakening within the script that corresponds to each one of us. So if the desire arises and the form of its expression does not hurt anyone, enjoy it while at the same time using the experience as the perfect curriculum to practice true forgiveness.

49 I have been told that I must be aware of my actions because they can affect other people.
Every decision that is made affects me alone. It affects nobody else because there is nobody! Remember that being only One (one mind), all "interaction" so to speak, is with oneself. Any decision that is made is not "my decision" but rather reflects the thought system with which the mind is identified. If I am

What Happened After Letting God

experiencing conflict, the mind is identified with the ego's thought system, therefore it is another forgiveness opportunity. If the mind is experiencing peace, there is nothing to do.

The more often you give yourself the opportunity to experience moments of stillness, taking advantage of every experience to practice true forgiveness (which is the same as saying choosing the Holy Spirit's thought system), every action that the character in the dream takes will be a reflection of his mind's decision for Truth. In reality, there is nothing to worry about because either way, every decision serves the awakening of consciousness. Nothing happens at random as the Manual for the Master of the Course reminds us: *"There are no accidents in salvation"*. M-3.1: 6. The fact that you have been led to read this book, or I should say, this kind of material, it is an indication that the mind is beginning to identify with a thought system that support its awakening. Therefore, your actions will start reflecting the mind's new decision for love through you.

50 *I wonder if this information could be explained to a child of three to ten years. To all the children that I know this information would be very confusing. How could I go about it?*
The information is only for you because it is your dream. You do not have to show it to "anybody". What you can do to teach a child is to live the principles you learn from the Course. The child will learn from your example, not from your words, or from what the books you want them to read. In due course, if they show any interest in this material, they will ask you. This will be a decision not taken by "you" or "them". It is a decision that takes place in the mind so that the mind can begin the awakening process.

51 *How is it possible that I can perceive oneness, unity, when my eyes are seeing separation? That being the case, how is it possible to practice unity? What did Jesus see when he was interacting with other people?*
The eyes of the body cannot see oneness because they only see separation. They only function to make the mind believe that it

is "seeing" differences. *A Course in Miracles* reminds us: "*Nothing the body's eyes seem to see can be anything but a form of temptation, since this was the purpose of the body itself*". W-pI.64.2:1. Let's go back to the dream analogy. When you sleep at night, there is only you and no one else in bed sleeping. When a dream is projected in your mind and you now believe that a "you" exists in the dream, what eyes are "seeing", those of the character that is inside the dream? Something or someone has to be "seeing" the images that are projected in the dream. So who or what is "seeing" those images? The answer is simple, the mind that is dreaming the dream.

At this level, even when it appears that we are bodies with eyes that "see", we can be aware that we are oneness, not as something that the eyes "see", or as something that we intellectually understand, but as an experience of love that surrounds everything that is experienced within the perceptual field. That would be the equivalent of the vision of Christ. We are reminded: "*Real vision is not only unlimited by space and distance, but it does not depend on the body's eyes at all*". W-pI.30.5:1.

True forgiveness prepares the mind for this experience. When we rest in this present moment, defocusing the mind from its fixed position on the objects appearing in its visual field, withdrawing all meaning, the mind, not the character, becomes aware that it is a mind and not a separate character. For this reason, the lessons of the Course begin with: "*Nothing I see... means anything*". W-pI.1. "*I have given everything I see...all the meaning that it has for me*" W-pI.2. "*I do not understand anything I see...*" W-pI.3. "*These thoughts do not mean anything...*" W-pI.4, and so on.

In this way, while the eyes of the body continue to perceive separate images, the mind experiences a sense of oneness, as if everything that I am apparently "seeing outside" is part of me. That is the closest thing to the oneness experience. It could be said then, that what Jesus "saw" when he was interacting with "other" people was the reflection of the unconditional love that was in the mind, without no disturbance from the images. A good analogy would be the cinema screen. The only thing that really exists is the blank screen. When a film is projected, the eyes are so distracted by the projected images that they overlook the fact that the only thing before them is a blank screen. If, at that moment, you defocus your attention from the images, you can observe the blank screen even when the images continue to be projected upon it.

We are not trying to practice or understand oneness. We are simply setting aside all interpretations of what we appear to be seeing, of what we appear to be feeling, of what we appear to be hearing, of what we appear to be perceiving, of what we appear to be imagining. This is how the experience of unity is revealed. Again, this is not a revelation by the senses, but an experience that cannot be explained or described. A sense of inner peace would be a description that our intellectual mind can comprehend. Do not try to have the experience because the search for experience is the negation of experience itself. This is completely frustrating for the mind that seeks, but perfectly simple for the mind that surrenders, lets go, and simply trusts.

52 How can I move around the world without judging?

The word judgment within this context has two meanings. The first is the judgment that has to do with what the eyes seem to be looking at, and the second has to do with the interpretation we make of what the eyes seem to be looking at. Let's look at it in the following way: all the objects that the body's eyes appear to "see" represent the world of separation. One body separated from another, a glass on the table, a flying plane, a tree in a forest, are all images that appear to be separated from one another. These images, like everything in the world of perception, are actually symbols that lack meaning. The problem is that if I told you to give me the symbol that is on top of the symbol to give it to the symbol, functionally speaking it would not help you and so we have to make judgment. Give me the glass (judgment) that is on the table (judgment) to give to my grandmother (judgment). They are judgments because they confirm the belief that the eyes are seeing separate symbols.

What is within our control is to stop projecting meaning onto those symbols. For example "That glass is dirty and who is the irresponsible one who failed to clean it?" or "I hate having to take this glass to my grandmother" are interpretations of symbols and actions that in themselves are completely neutral. When you stop condemning (stop judging) you invite the mind to stay in a state of peace and perfect equanimity without disturbance from the judgments that must be made in order to function at the level of this apparent world. We could substitute the word judgment for condemnation in which case the question would become: How can I move around the world without condemning? The answer is simple, to stop projecting meaning onto everything. In a word, forgiving.

53 If everything I see is a reflection of me (as part of the same mind), does this mean that the way others act or feel is a representation of what is in me?
First of all, "I", like "you", like "everyone", are all part of a projection that takes place in the mind that dreams all of "us". Therefore none of "us" as "individuals" projects anything. Consequently we are not responsible for what "others" do or say. They are simply projected images perceived. What I feel when perceiving these images is a representation, not necessarily of what is in me, but a representation of the thought system with which the mind is identified. In that sense one could say that what I see "outside" is a representation of what is in me, as a mind, not as a body. *A Course in Miracles* states it this way: "*As you look in* (as the mind looks in, not you as a persona), *you* (the mind) *choose the guide for seeing* (ego or Holy Spirit). *And then you* (the mind) *look out and behold his witnesses*". T-12. VII: 7: 2-3.

So you could say that there are two levels. The first level is that of wanting to see a world of separation. This is what takes place in the mind that dreams this dream, not in us as characters. Thus what I desire, as mind, is what I perceive. The second level has to do with how the mind wants to interpret the world it is perceiving. The first level of projection could be said to be automatic. When I wake up in the morning I am experiencing myself as a body, a projection is experienced which is immediately justified by perception. What I see, what I feel, what I hear, what I think, all seem to be automatic. Once the projection is perceived, a system of thoughts with which to interpret the images can be chosen. If the ego's thought system is chosen, the images will be used to keep the mind distracted. If the Holy Spirit's thought system (true forgiveness) is chosen, each experience will serve a different purpose, to make the mind aware that it is dreaming a dream.

The Course tells us: *"Yet we have learned that the Holy Spirit has another use for all the illusions you have made, and therefore He sees another purpose in them. To the Holy Spirit, the world is a place where you learn to forgive yourself what you think of as your sins. In this perception, the physical appearance of temptation becomes the spiritual recognition of salvation"*. W-pI.64.2: 2-4.

Now images are still perceived: some say some things and some say other thing; some feel one way and others feel differently; and some act in one way and some act in different ways. Yet now we are at peace with what is, recognizing the only thing that is real in each and every one of the scenarios that are presented is the love of God.

54 If I am reacting while someone is yelling at me how can I perceive love, knowing that love is the only thing that is real?
The phrasing of this question makes the experience of love impossible. This is because in reacting to someone who screams, the obstacle to love is more real to us than love itself, although Love is what we are. The real answer to this question requires us to open ourselves up to the corrective thought system of the Holy Spirit, using Course tools such as *"I am never upset for the reason I think"* W-pI.5 or *"I am determined to see things differently"* W-pI.21 or *"Above all else I want to see things differently"* W-pI.28 or *"I do not know what anything, including this, means. And

so I do not know how to respond to it. And I will not use my own past learning as the light to guide me now". T-14.XI.6: 6-9. I could cite many passages from the Course whose purpose is to help release the mind from the ego's tight grip.

Obviously, these are just words that in and of themselves do not have the power to effect a change in mentality. But they serve to support the inner work that is being done which is to open ourselves fully to feel those feelings that are emerging without justifying them. That is the most difficult part of the work and yet it is the bridge that must be crossed so that love can be recognized. Once I am aware of what is actually taking place in me, I can see what is taking place in "others."

By setting aside any interpretation that the mind formulates to justify whatever it is I am feeling, I am allowing the Holy Spirit to change my perception. As a result, I can become aware of the love that I am. Instead of feeling attacked, I recognize that there is no such thing as a person attacking "me". It is nothing more and nothing less than a call for love. I am the sane part of the mind that unconsciously demonstrates to "everyone" that they have access to the same thought system. That's what Jesus did, showing us by example that we all have access to the same thought system he chose.

55 What to do when one is trapped in "the dark night of the soul"?

The Christian mystic San Juan de la Cruz talks about the dark night of the soul. *A Course in Miracles* refers, not necessarily to the dark night of the soul, but to the internal conflict that is generated when the ego's thought system (our false identity) is being undone. Here are two excerpts from the Course that talk about this process. One is: *"As this recognition becomes more firmly established, it becomes a turning point. This ultimately reawakens spiritual vision, simultaneously weakening the investment in physical sight. The alternating investment in the two levels of perception is usually experienced as conflict, which can become very acute. But the outcome is as certain as God"*. T-2.III.3: 7-10

The other: *"And now you stand in terror before what you swore never to look upon. Your eyes look down, remembering your promise to your "friends." The "loveliness" of sin, the delicate appeal of guilt, the "holy" waxen image of death, and the fear of vengeance of the ego you swore in blood not to desert, all rise and bid you not to raise your eyes. For you realize that if you look on this and let the veil be lifted, they will be gone forever. All of your "friends," your "protectors" and your "home" will vanish. Nothing that you remember now will you remember"*. T-19.IV.D.6: 1-6

This conflict tends to arise because of the mind's desire to experience itself as a Totality, as Love, as Oneness, while simultaneously fearing to let go of its false identity as a separate self. It would be like the worm that feels the call to be a butterfly, only he would have to let go of his cocoon. Imagining the worm to have an intellectual mind, this would terrify him since his identity as a worm is the only thing he knows. In other words, he believes that he will "die" when in reality he will be liberated!

When the mind begins to open up to a much more expansive experience, one that goes beyond the limitations that have been imposed upon it, an identity crisis may be experienced. All my life I have believed myself to be a person, a separate individual. That's who "I am" and I have been defending it at all costs! What happens when the question arises: What if that is not true? Sometimes this awakening of consciousness can take the form of depression, apathy, sadness. An internal conflict is generated because any belief about what we are flies in the face of the experience we are going through. We think we are going crazy when in reality, all that is happening is that the mind is beginning to regain its sanity.

I'm not implying that everyone will experience such a transition in the same way. Some people may not experience any pain or suffering. What is clear is that for the mind to heal from its belief in separation it has to be willing to let go of every belief and every concept learned about the world, about our experience, about who we are, about life in general. This letting go of all we have learned, which constitutes who I think I am, from the ego´s perspective is a form of death, and therefore it is frightening. The Manual for Teachers of the Course says: *"First, they must go through what might be called "a period of undoing." This need not be painful, but it usually is so experienced"*. M-4.I.A.3: 1-2. Another excerpt from the Course tells us: *"The beginning phases of this reversal are often quite painful, for as blame is withdrawn from without, there is a strong tendency to harbor it within. It is difficult at first to realize that this is exactly the same thing, for there is no distinction between within and without"*. T-11.IV.4:5-6.

Ultimately there is nothing we can do but "die" which has nothing to do with "committing suicide" or the death of the body. It has to do with allowing every feeling, every thought, every sensation to be without any resistance in order to be "born again", meaning for the mind to be returned to its natural state of peace. In this context, being born again makes perfect sense. Saint Francis of Assisi said, "... it is in pardoning that we are pardoned. And it's in dying that we are born to eternal life.

56 How to approach the death of a loved one?

When the mind is aware of its reality, the images in the dream are recognized as transient scenes that constantly appear and disappear (are born and die). The loss of a loved one does not mean any more the loss of a pair of shoes. *A Course in Miracles* reminds us that there are no hierarchies of illusions: *"This principle evolves from the belief there is a hierarchy of illusions; some are more valuable and therefore true"*. T-23.II.2:3.

The suffering we feel when a loved one leaves this physical plane is based on the belief that I am a body that it is born and can die. I project the fear of dying onto other bodies. The practice of true forgiveness makes me aware that what I am is mind. The fear of letting go of the body disappears in the recognition that death does not exist. When a loved one leaves the body, I know that body is not what he or she really is and so my peace is unaffected by the event.

This does not mean that sometimes you don't miss the presence of a loved one due to the fact that you were both relating as bodies. Nevertheless even if the memory awakens a feeling of sadness at the psychological level, there is no suffering.

Like everything else, awakening is a process, an apprenticeship. Some lessons certainly appear to be more difficult to embrace than others, such as the loss of a loved one. We begin by practicing how to forgive the simple. We have to apply it to each and every one of the experiences that somehow, however subtly, seem to disturb our peace. An example would be the frustration or anger that can come when you are looking for an object in your house and you cannot find it. When you ask your daughter or son to put the clothes in the laundry basket and they fail to do it. When you want to watch a TV show and the phone rings and it's the bank and now you have to answer the call. Or when the children argue and there is no way to keep them quiet. The list of examples is endless.

If true forgiveness is not practiced daily, we are not training the mind. And when a difficult situation arises, one which the world of illusions sees as devastating, it will consume us. This is why I want to emphasize that this process must be dedicated to remembering Truth, not solving worldly issues. If not, forgiveness will be employed as a magic wand to feel better, to eradicate the pain, to fix problems in the dream instead of freeing the mind. This approach to forgiveness simply increases unconscious guilt, solidifying the belief in separation.

57 I do not understand what is meant by a divided mind since God is all that exists.
God is the only thing that exists. There is nothing else! There is no "divided" mind, there is no "dream", there is no "separation", there is no "I", there is no "world". It's just that when we experience ourselves as bodies "living" in a "world" of "separation" we try to find an explanation so that this experience can at least make sense. And although nothing has happened, a story is told that is used within a frame of reference that the mind can at least accept, so that it can open itself to

the practice of true forgiveness. The story says that within the Only Thing that Exists (God), a thought appears. This is what we know as mind or consciousness (lowercase). This mind, this consciousness seems to divide itself. Let's look at the following image:

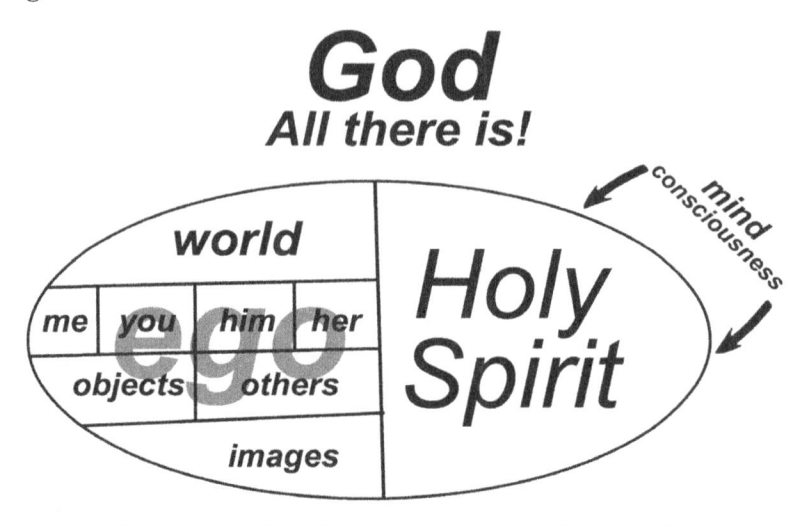

God
All there is!

world — me | you | him | her — objects | others — ego — images — Holy Spirit — mind consciousness

The mind (lowercase) is the experience of the ego (separation). Within that mind, the ego subdivides the mind (projects a dream of separation within the mind). In that same mind, that same consciousness rests the Holy Spirit (God's response to the apparent separation). Returning to the original question of how separation is possible if God is the only thing that exists, this represents the great paradox. If you try to make rational sense of it you will end up running round in circles. The Course says: "The ego will demand many answers that this Course does not give. It does not recognize as questions the mere form of a question to which an answer is impossible. The ego may ask, "How did the impossible occur?", *"To what did the impossible happen?"* (how can the mind be divided is God is all there is), *and may ask this in many forms. Yet there is no answer; only an experience. Seek only this, and do not let theology delay you"*. C-In.4: 1-5. The important thing is to exercise your only function, which is to forgive, and observe the restoration of peace in the mind as the unconscious guilt is being eradicated.

58 Now that I have become a dedicated student of A Course in Miracles, I feel that I do not belong anywhere, as if I have nothing in common with others. Can you offer any suggestions on how to deal with that?

First of all, you have nothing in common with others at the level of form. But if you have something in common with everyone it would be that in essence we are the same. None of us feels that we belong here, although some have failed to recognize it. *A Course in Miracles* tells us: *"This world you seem to live in is not home to you. And somewhere in your mind you know that this is true"*. W-pI.182.1:1-2. At first, being so identified with the ego's thought system, all our relationships serve to sustain this false identity. In fact, this world was made to sustain it. Nevertheless, there is no reason to despair because the only thing that changes is that every experience that affects our peace of mind is used as an opportunity to practice true forgiveness.

As the mind becomes empty of content, as it stops projecting meaning (unconscious guilt) onto to each experience, we begin to relate to the world from another space. We are no longer in conflict with the world. Quite the opposite: we are at peace; we no longer need to feel special, to feel loved and accepted because this peace is self-generated. We now relate to people without the need to change them or to adhere to any specific point of view. The result is that we enjoy their company and, in turn, they enjoy ours because they experience themselves as accepted in our presence. They feel they are being heard, they feel comfortable with us. Who would not want to be with you if, in your presence, they feel accepted, they experience peace, they can be who they really are without the need to pretend? They feel free!

I may be deviating a bit from the question but this story came to mind and I would like to share it. It is about a wise man who was said to have discovered the secret of happiness. A journalist looking for an interview had a chance to ask him, "People say that you are always happy, they say that you have found the secret to happiness. Is that true?" The wise man replied,

"I do not understand your question because I honestly do not know what secret you are talking about". Then the journalist suggested, "Let's do one thing, will you allow me to stay with you for a few days and observe your behavior to see if maybe I can deduce why people say you have found the secret to happiness?" The sage replied, " Sure." The journalist observed that a person arrived and shared something, then asked for the wise man´s opinion. The wise man said, "I agree with you, you are absolutely right". The person left happy while the wise man happily continued with his life. Then another person arrived who shared with the wise man a point of view completely opposite to that of the previous person and asked the wise man for his opinion. The wise man answered, "I agree with you, you are absolutely right." As the wise man agreed with everyone, he did not experience conflict. The journalist said, "If you agree with everyone, if you do not express your point of view, does not that make you a conformist, an unreliable person?" to which the wise man answered, "no, it makes me a happy person."

If you were to identify with your nature as Totality, then wherever you are, with or without company, you would never experience loneliness. How could God feel "alone" if God is all there is? And "you" being a part of God (Totality), wherever you are and whomever you are with, feels like home. What a happy way to live!

59 What would A Course in Miracles say about homosexuality? Absolutely nothing because the Course never addresses bodies. It only addresses the mind. The Holy Spirit does not pay attention to what takes place in the world because nothing is happening in the world. What takes place in the world is part of a script projected by the ego with the purpose of keeping the mind closed off from Truth. Whatever the sexual orientation of any individual, in the eyes of God, he or she remains the Holy Child of God, innocent, free from all guilt and unconditionally loved.

In this sense homosexual, heterosexual, bisexual, transsexual, or any derivative of those labels do not affect our identity as Love. We need only remember our one function, which is to forgive.

60 I have heard that when one goes to sleep and begins to dream, that is the space in which the soul plays because it has been released from the body. Is it like that?
The body is simply a projection of the mind, of consciousness and so a body that does not exist cannot have a "soul". There may, though, be dreams within dreams within dreams ad infinitum.

"We" for example, are now being dreamt by consciousness, by the mind. However, when "we" lay in bed at night, it seems that now "we" are the ones who dream, and another movie (dream) is projected within our mind, very similar to the one we are experiencing now. Only it is governed by different laws. In this experience there is the law of gravity, in our dreams there is no such law. In this one we can die, in our dreams we cannot. But no matter the story unfolding in either dream, the objective is to keep the mind distracted from Truth, from Love, from God by keeping its attention on the content of each dream.

61 How do I know if it is the voice of the ego or the Holy Spirit that I am listening to?
When we speak of the "Voice" of the Holy Spirit or the "voice" of the ego, we are not necessarily speaking of a "voice" that tells us with words what to do or what not to do. Still, the Holy Spirit can take the form that is necessary for His message to reach a mind that is open and receptive. When inner peace is experienced, it is an indication that we are identified with the Holy Spirit's thought system. Conversely, when we are experiencing fear, it is obvious that we are identified with the ego's thought system. And they both offer an interpretation. The question therefore could be changed to: How do I know if the interpretation of each experience is in accordance that of the Holy Spirit or the ego? The Holy Spirit's interpretation always leads to a state of inner peace. It's that simple!

Also remember that the ego always leads the mind to identify with a separate "I". The Holy Spirit´s voice, or interpretation, leads the mind to experience itself as the space that contains this "I", that observes it and does not identify with it. That is why peace is experienced when the identification is with the Holy Spirit´s thought system.

62 Is there what might be called a "healthy" or "benevolent" ego?
A "healthy" or "benevolent" ego would be as contradictory as saying a benign terminal illness, or a light darkness. The direct answer is no, because the ego is simply a belief whose sole purpose is to keep the mind distracted from Truth. If it were not for the belief in the mind in an ego, this world of separation would not exist so there would no "I" or a "you" or an "all". The ego is simply the denial of Reality. You can deny Reality all you like by continuing to choose the ego's thought system, but the Reality in God remains forever intact. *A Course in Miracles* reminds us: *"The ego is nothing more than a part of your belief about yourself. Your other life has continued without interruption, and has been and always will be totally unaffected by your attempts to dissociate it"*. T-4.VI.1: 6-7. Best thing would be to live our "normal" life, allowing the ego to simply be, making sure we don't overlook our only function which is to forgive.

63 I've heard a lot about gratitude; that if I want my life to change I have to be grateful. And yet, no matter how grateful I try to be, most of the time my life does not seem to improve.
When you try to use gratitude so that the character's life "improves" it is used for the benefit of the ego in order to keep the mind distracted from Truth. A state of true gratitude has more to do with the recognition at all times of our reality in God. The more we become aware of this, the more we settle into a state of permanent gratitude.

64 How does the Course in Miracles see the idea of positive thinking?
The moment an evaluation is made, a personal interpretation,

"positive" or "negative, bars the way to inner peace. *A Course in Miracles* is about experiencing inner peace, not about thinking one way or another. The first thing to be aware of, difficult as this might be to recognize, is that every thought is neutral. No thought has the power to affect my inner peace. Only when I label it as "positive" or "negative", when I interpret it, does my peace seesaw between two polarities, pain and pleasure. The Course simply encourages the mind to put aside any kind of evaluation about what I am thinking, what I am feeling, about everything that is being perceived. That's why it says: *"You do not know the meaning of anything you perceive. Not one thought you hold is wholly true. The recognition of this is your firm beginning"*. T-11.VIII.3:1-3. This recognition is what quietens the mind long enough to see its reality as mind, as consciousness and not as a separate body. This has nothing to do with thinking "positive". It is complete liberation from thinking. Thoughts continue to arise but they will have no effect on our inner peace.

65 What is it to be a teacher of God? A teacher of God is the individual who demonstrates the pri
nciples that the Course teaches. That is why the Manual for the Teacher tells us that: *"to teach is to demonstrate."* M-In.2:1. When we speak of being a teacher of God, we must be aware that the Course is not talking to the character "I" who believes itself to be here, but to the mind that is dreaming me. Otherwise what typically happens is a confusion of levels.

To explain further, if being a teacher of God meant going around in the world teaching *A Course in Miracles*, then the Course would be contradicting itself when it tells us that "There is no world! This is the central thought the Course attempts to teach". W-pI.32.6: 2. It is rather to observe in each moment whether one is identified with the ego´s thought system or with the Holy Spirit´s. Whichever thought system is chosen will determine what is true for that individual who will act accordingly. This is what I will 'teach' because this is what I am demonstrating.

Let's look at what the Manual for the Teacher tells us about what it is to be a teacher of God: *"There are only two thought systems, and you demonstrate that you believe one or the other is true all the time. From your demonstration others learn, and so do you"*. M-In.2: 2-3. So at all times we are all teaching (demonstrating). The Teacher of God is constantly identified with the thought system of the Holy Spirit. There is an excerpt from the Course where Jesus, referring to this says: *"I have nothing that does not come from God. The difference between us now is that I have nothing else"*. T-1.II.3: 11-12

66 What does the Course mean when it says "infinite patience produces immediate effects (T-5.VI.12: 1)"?
Infinite patience could be said to be synonymous with trust. When there is trust, there is peace. If I trust, I have all the patience in the world and so I experience peace at all times. That is the immediate result. The ego's thought system, which only believes in time and space, assumes that what we are being told is that if I want something in the world and I have infinite patience I will experience that result eventually. What it does is direct the attention of the mind to the world of dreams and, therefore, keep it distracted from Truth.

67 How to receive the guidance of the Holy Spirit?
The ego's thought system has the dual version of how to receive guidance. It assumes that there is a self in the world that now asks for guidance for something abstract; to know what to say or what to do in the dream. In the dream there is nothing to say or to do because the dream is just that, a projection. So from a purely non-dual perspective, receiving guidance would be the equivalent of being completely open to the present moment, free of personal interpretations, free of expectations. In this way, peace is restored. From this space, free from fear, it can be deduced that whatever is being done or said in each moment comes from Holy Spirit's guidance. I, for example, do not feel "guided" to write these words. It is simply what is happening in my script. If I am not at peace, regardless of what I do or not do, it can be said that I am being "guided" by the ego's thought system.

68 If the ego is a belief, and all beliefs can be changed, can I not then change the belief that I am, or that I have an ego with the belief that I am one with God and, therefore, eradicate the ego completely?

What happens is that the ego is itself a belief in the mind and this is where all beliefs derive. When in the mind the belief of an ego arises, a world is projected (dream) and inside the dream I believe that I am a character with all its beliefs. Trying to "change" a belief from the character's perspective only reinforces the belief that a character exists. It is a dead end because I have to forget that I am God to believe myself to be a character. So all this physical experience only endorses the belief in the physical experience. See the trap?

As the mind experiences silence as a result of the practice of true forgiveness, it becomes more aware of itself as mind, and the character is no longer an interference. It is just an experience. Then everything is viewed as an experience. For example, "I" as a character do not write these words. The experience of writing seems to be happening. "I" as a character do not see anything. The experience of seeing seems to be happening. "I" as a character do not hear anything. The experience of hearing seems to be happening. "I" as a character do not feel anything. The experience of feeling seems to be happening. "I" as a character do not think anything. The experience of thinking seems to be happening. This last sentence reminds me of the excerpt from the Course that says: *"It is because the thoughts you think you think appear as images that you do not recognize them as nothing. You think you think them, and so you think you see them. This is how your "seeing" was made. This is the function you have given your body's eyes. It is not seeing"*. W-pI.15.1: 1-5.

So "I", as a character, do not have beliefs. The beliefs seem to be happening to "me". A semi-awake mind, so to speak, is a mind that is aware that it is consciousness. Therefore, I (the mind) have to open myself to each experience, without analyzing it. Setting aside all personal interpretations, I allow only the Holy Spirit's interpretation to take place, which is what happens when I recognize that I know nothing. As the disidentification with the character progresses, that which is more in accordance with my true essence (inner peace) begins to take first position in the mind. This experience can only take place when all beliefs are undone. And that is the curriculum that *A Course in Miracles* poses: the undoing of all beliefs. So it says: *"Hold back but one belief, one offering, and love is gone, because you asked a substitute to take its place"*. T-24.I.1: 4

69 When babies are born, are they born innocent?

The common belief is that babies are born "innocent" and as they grow up, based on what they are taught, their ego develops, causing them to lose their innocence. According to *A Course in Miracles*, the ego is a belief that takes place in the mind, in consciousness. This belief is what projects the world of form. The world of form is this physical experience where apparently human beings are "born", have an "experience of life" and finally "die".

When a baby is "born" (ego projecting an image), being ego, (and I did not say "his ego", I said that because he is ego), the baby´s ego is 100% developed, just like an "adult's". But to keep the language consistent with the question, the ego of a newborn baby is no different than yours or mine. What happens is that if we take a newborn child, not free of ego, but free of beliefs, his behavior will reflect the belief system that he or she consciously or unconsciously has chosen to adopt. If a newborn baby is raised in a family where "healthy" beliefs are inculcated, it could be said, although this is not guaranteed, that it is more likely to function in a healthy way in society. If, on the other hand, the same baby is raised in a dysfunctional family, it is more likely, although not guaranteed, that its behavior in society will reflect that dysfunctionality. Why in both cases did I claim, "although not guaranteed?" This is because the script is already written, and each has his forgiveness opportunities laid out.

A Course in Miracles aims to undo all beliefs before undoing the foundational belief that says, "I am a body (separate entity)".

But since the separation from God never occurred, regardless of what I believe about myself, I am, and will always be innocent, which has nothing to do with being a "baby" but because of Who I Am.

70 If I put the Course into practice, can I heal my body?

First, let's see how *A Course in Miracles* defines the body: *"The body is a fence the Son of God imagines he has built, to separate parts of his Self from other parts. It is within this fence he thinks he lives, to die as it decays and crumbles. For within this fence he thinks that he is safe from love. Identifying with his safety, he regards himself as what his safety is. How else could he be certain he remains within the body, keeping love outside?"* W-pII.5.1: 1-5.

When a body gets sick, it is no different than a leaf from a tree falling to the ground, or a wave in the ocean breaking against a stone, or a child asking his mother for ice cream etc. In other words, since there is no hierarchy of illusions, what would be the reason for wanting to sustain a body, healthy or sick? The ego thought system would be the one that wants to find a way to "heal" a body. Having said that, let us also be aware that the body is a projection of the mind. Unconscious guilt might take the form of projecting some kind of sickness onto a body.

The practice of true forgiveness places the mind in the service of Truth. This leads to the eradication of unconscious guilt which could, in turn, result in a body that is cured from a sickness. As the Course emphasizes: *"The "self" that needs protection is not real. The body, valueless and hardly worth the least defense, need merely be perceived as quite apart from you, and it becomes a healthy, serviceable instrument through which the mind can operate until its usefulness is over. Who would want to keep it when its usefulness is done?"* W-pI.135.8: 1-3.

Always remember that if the mind's focus is on a body being "cured", its attention is on illusions and away from Truth. It is holding on to unconscious guilt, which is the reason why a "body exists". The focus is not in "healing" a "body" but on healing the mind from the belief that it is a body. When the mind identifies with its essence as Totality, the mind is in absolute and imperturbable peace with what is, and what takes place with the body becomes completely irrelevant. Returning to the analogy of the dream, if at night I am dreaming that the body is sick, and I am aware that it is only a dream, what takes place within this projected body is no longer important. The goal of *A Course in Miracles* is to restore peace in the mind, not to do interfere with the body. In the meantime, we do whatever we feel inspired to do to take care of the body, knowing that it is not "us" who are doing anything, it is simply what's taking place in the moment.

71 Does intuition exist?
According to the ego's thought system intuition is a "sense", lacking in logic, that serves to "supposedly help" us to "choose" between "different" alternatives. Intuition itself is a memory, conscious or unconscious, that is activated in certain scenarios and is somatized in the body as a feeling that keeps the mind distracted from the Truth. In this sense what we call "intuition" is only a distracting mechanism. From a non-dual point of view intuition would be the equivalent to the virtue of discerning between that which is real and that which is false.

Remember that being a dreamed character, I do not really have the ability to "choose". It is the mind that dreams "me", that chooses based on a script that is already written. I can only observe the "decisions" that in every moment are being made through the "me" character by the mind that is dreaming "me".

It cannot be denied that because there seems to be an "I" experiencing feelings that feel "better" than others, these feelings appear to have an influence in the decision making process. This is where the concept of intuition comes to play. If a decision feels "right" it is considered to be a "correct" one. If, on the other hand, the decision feels "wrong", it is considered to be an "incorrect" one. Yet, how many decisions were made, that initially felt "wrong", and maybe even guilt-inducing, ended up being the best decisions? Similarly, how many decisions that initially felt "right" were later shown to be not necessarily the best choice? This is reminiscent of the following excerpt from the Course. While I am not saying it is referring to the world of form, I like to use it to highlight this issue: *"Some of your greatest advances you have judged as failures, and some of your deepest retreats you have evaluated as success"*. T-18.V.1: 6

I prefer not to use the concept of intuition in order to generate further confusion. As I see it, my job is to simply observe how easily the mind can be distracted by choosing the ego's thought system over that of the Holy Spirit's. This will determine whether I react to the world of illusions or not, whether I am playing the game as if I am "choosing" according to how I "feel" instead of being pulled into it. In my case, I trust that whatever decision ends up being made is the one that had to be made, and use it as the curriculum to exercise my only function, which is to forgive.

72 What does the Course mean when it says: Do not fight against yourself?
The question is based on this excerpt from the Course: *"And if you find resistance strong and dedication weak, you are not ready. Do not fight yourself"*. T-30.In.1: 6-7

When the process of undoing our personal identity (ego) begins, life presents scenarios that cause us to begin questioning every belief that we hold. This is not done to create suffering but to free the mind from its very imprisonment, a prison created by holding on to any belief we have about life, about ourselves, about anything. Total acceptance of life as it happens equates to the practice of forgiveness and re-establishes peace in the mind. If there is a very strong identification, conscious or unconscious, with any belief, we don't fight against it since opposing it simply strengthens the ego's thought system, perpetuating the suffering.

Although a Course, being a non-dual teaching, refers to the mind's resistance to Truth, I would like to use a worldly example. When Fayna and I started living together her two children were fourteen years of age. Although in theory I was very clear that the world has no power to affect my peace, the dynamics of a family relationship with children showed that there was still a lot of unconscious resistance in me.

We sat down to talk as we usually did and I shared my concerns. Although leaving the relationship is not the "solution" to the problem, the Course does not ask me to stay. The Course does not ask me to sacrifice. It simply exhorts me to at least acknowledge, even intellectually, that the world is not the "cause" of any lack of peace. As life presents one scenario after another, all I have to do is remember my only function, which is to forgive. As every scenario is forgiven, only love will spring forth from me, for that is the only thing I will perceive.

However, in that particular scenario, respecting the fact that at the time I was not ready for the demands and responsibility that involved dealing with children that age, the most loving thing for me to do was to leave the relationship as opposed to try to fight against myself by attempting to ignore what I was feeling, justifying it or covering it up with, "I have to force myself to be here and forgive..." That is not forgiveness, that would be torture.

73 What does A Course in Miracles mean when it says that the curriculum is highly individualized?
Going back to the analogy of the dream, only one mind dreaming a dream within which there appear to be "many" parts, the concept of "individualized" makes no sense. Yet in the dream, where there appears to be a "you," a "me," a "them," "you" experience yourself as an "individual". "I" experience myself as an "individual". In the same way "they" are experiencing themselves as "many individuals". Whilst in reality there is no such thing as "we" experiencing ourselves as "individuals", the dreaming mind through each of the "parts" experiences a sense of "individuality". But since "I" (Nick Arandes) as well as "you" (whatever your name is) experience ourselves as "separate" individuals, each of "us" has a curriculum. Now,

in the dreaming mind, there is the memory that reminds the mind through each of the parts that its reality is God, Unity, not separate individuals (parts). That memory (Holy Spirit), being in charge of the curriculum of the mind itself, is simultaneously in charge of each of the parts. This is known as: *"... God's plan for salvation!"* T-12.I.6:4.

A Course in Miracles simply exhorts the mind to direct its attention to this memory, while the curriculum for each of the "individuals" unfolds as it is going to unfold. The Course reminds us: *"The program of studies is highly individualized, and all its aspects are under the care and special direction of the Holy Spirit. This is His responsibility, and He alone is qualified to assume it."* M-29.2: 6..8.

74 What is love?

If I use the word Love (uppercase) we are talking about Truth, what is Real, in other words, God. This world of separation in which we pretend to live is known as the denial of Love. The denial of God. The denial of the Kingdom. Therefore we cannot speak here of True Love. We can speculate about It, but the experience of True Love would be the disappearance of its opposite, which once again, is this experience of separation. We can, however, question the concepts we have about Love so that we can open ourselves to an experience that at least points in that direction. So, let's play a little with the words.

If I asked you: What is happiness?, you could surely share your opinion. If I ask the same question to another person and an opinion arises that is in opposition to yours, which of the two answers would be "correct"? The answer is, neither. For that answer to be true, it has to be absolute, it has to be the same for everyone, i.e. for all of the parts. Truth (uppercase), God, Love, again, is absolute. It is the same for all of the parts, for the One Mind. It has no opposites. That is why in the introduction of *A Course in Miracles* we are told: *"The opposite of love is fear, but what is all-encompassing can have no opposite"*. T-In.1: 8.

So if God is Love, and Love is the only thing that exists, what would have to happen for all of us to experience that same Love? To be in agreement with a universal concept? Could that be possible? Or would it then be more practical for everyone to let go of their concept of what Love is? Returning to the question, what is Love?, I don't know. We cannot define what we are, but we can be aware of what we are not. Hence the Course emphasizes that: *"The Course does not aim at teaching the meaning of love, for that is beyond what can be taught. It does aim, however, at removing the blocks to the awareness of love's presence, which is your natural inheritance"*. T-In.1: 6-7.

The closest thing to the Love that we are, which in turn can be experienced in our physical experience, is peace. In that sense, the word love is used in lowercase. Peace is what allows me to relate to all my brothers from a place of love. If I believe that love is a feeling, a sensation, a desire for pleasure, now I invite all kinds of conflict. Feelings of jealousy are justified when we say they arise because of the "love" one feels towards someone else. There are those who even kill in the name of "love". We suffer for "love" and others sacrifice for "love". Erotic products are sold to enhance "love". Some people are punished in the name of "love"; the list is endless. The only purpose of true forgiveness is to remove all the obstacles that we have placed before the love that we are.

I remember having had experiences of a love that cannot be described with words since what True Love (God) is cannot be limited to concepts. They have not been pleasurable experiences. Rather they have always been accompanied by an indescribable sense of peace and serenity. Looking in retrospect, after deep investigation, what those experiences have had in common is that in the mind there was no judgment (condemnation) whatsoever. To my understanding, the best definition of Love I can offer is to live the present experience, free of all judgment, in total acceptance of what is.

Conclusion

As our journey together draws to an end, I would like to clarify something. My last book, *'What happens when you let God'* has very useful content for someone who is embarking on a path towards remembering Truth. The book you are reading now is one I wrote for myself to further clarify the purely non-dual nature of the teachings of *A Course in Miracles*. With this in mind I have done all I can to keep the non-dual message of the Course intact. Nothing has been written with the intention of selling a book or making the Course´s message more attractive or more appealing. Every word contained in this book has been written in a way that I would like it to be explained to me, so that I can take full advantage of Jesus or Holy Spirit´s message in His Course.

In the second part of this book I answered every question with complete honesty and according to my understanding of the material. I recognize that some of the answers may generate resistance. Not all of us want to let go of our personal identity in favor of Truth, even if sooner or later we will have to respond to His call. I always like to refer to these two quotes of the Course: *"Tolerance for pain may be high, but it is not without limit. Eventually everyone begins to recognize, however dimly, that there must be a better way"*. T-2.III.3: 5-6. And: *"If you want to be like me I will help you, knowing that we are alike. If you want to be different, I will wait until you change your mind"*. T-8.IV.6: 3-4.

Please do not use this book as a substitute for the Course. No matter how honest my desire to keep the message of the Course intact, or how clear my understanding of the material may be, the Course has a highly individualized curriculum (*"The curriculum is highly individualized, and all aspects are under the Holy Spirit's particular care and guidance"*) M-29.2: 6. Designed by the Only Teacher who can teach it, we are reminded: *"On this journey you have chosen me as your companion instead of the ego.*

Do not attempt to hold on to both, or you will try to go in different directions and will lose the way". T-8.V.5: 8-9.

Should you choose to study *A Course in Miracles*, my only suggestion would be that you give it the time and dedication it deserves. As the Course states: *"This is a Course in mind training. All learning involves attention and study at some level. Some of the later parts of the Course rest too heavily on these earlier sections not to require their careful study. You will also need them for preparation. Without this, you may become much too fearful of what is to come to make constructive use of it. However, as you study these earlier sections, you will begin to see some of the implications that will be amplified later on"*. T-1.VII.4: 1-6

In addition to the textbook, the Course contains a Workbook for Students dictated by the Holy Spirit, or Jesus and is a one-year curriculum for mind training. It is not one-year's work. It is a life-long process. In the epilogue we are reminded: *"This Course is a beginning, not an end"*. W-Epilogue.1: 1.

Remember that the thought system to which we are faithfully attached and do not want to release, even when it is so painful, is being undone. This attachment is the cause of all suffering. In addition, when we begin this journey towards Truth, the ego's thought system that we tenaciously hold onto will show its true face, with the possible intensification of fear and terror.

I recognize that these words do not seem very encouraging on the surface. On a deeper level, *A Course in Miracles* is very kind and lovingly exposing the ego's thought system - how it operates, how we have constructed it and the reason we continue to hold on to it - so that we can let it go. We may not want to look at the obstacles to peace, preferring to focus on the nice parts of the Course like when it talks about love. That is why the only Teacher who can lead us to the recognition of our True Nature is Jesus, the Holy Spirit, or whatever name you choose so long as you don't invest anything in the symbol. If the desire for Truth is firmly rooted, we must be willing to look at everything we have placed before Love, and the Workbook takes us by the hand. If you feel moved to study *A Course in Miracles*, the publisher is 'The Foundation for Inner Peace', and the link to its website is: www. acim.org where you can order a copy. You can also get it at most bookstores.

I cannot say with certainty why I found myself sharing the theory of the Course through talks and writings. It was never something I set out to do. It was simply what happened. Yet, looking back, I can see how sharing the Course´s teachings has made it easier for me to keep the message present so that I can continue applying it, integrating it, and in the best possible way, living it. During all these years, the understanding has deepened. This implies that some of the content I thought I understood about the Course was not fully accurate. I dare say that as long as I continue experiencing myself as a body, there will always be forgiveness opportunities. I am aware that the true practice of the Course is reflected in the attitude of the practitioner, not in his theoretical understanding. If love is what´s being extended, if peace is what´s being extended, if understanding, kindness is what being extended, *A Course in Miracles* has been integrated. That´s why its been said: *"Wherefore by their fruits ye shall know them"*. [Matthew 7:20].

How do you know if you are in that space? The Course puts it this way: *"You have one test, as sure as God, by which to recognize if what you learned is true. If you are wholly free of fear of any kind, and if all those who meet or even think of you share in your perfect peace, then you can be sure that you have learned God's lesson, and not your own"*. T -14.XI.5: 1-2. When you read *A Course in Miracles*, regardless of whether the text is understood or not, it cannot be denied that there is a transcendental love that at times takes the mind to a state of peace that is not of this world.

Although I am aware that I never know anything, as I continue looking at the unconscious guilt in order to heal the mind, I will probably continue to give talks and write about my experiences, always doing my best to recognize that ultimately there are no differences between us. *A Course in Miracles* may be my personal path, but everyone can choose what they want to do with the Course, which is what will take place anyway. Any teaching, being subject to interpretation according to the teacher chosen by the mind, serves to increase separation or encourage unity. For many years, consciously or unconsciously, I ended up experiencing separation by defending the Course's theory instead of living it, even when the Course itself reminds me: *"And truth needs no defense..."* T-26.VII.8:2.

If sharing *A Course in Miracles* is what the script has in store for me, I trust in God's plan for salvation. Aside from that, I do not know what I may end up doing in this "world". All I know is that my only function is to forgive, even when forgiving is something that is not in my control. If there is no "me" then who is the one who can exercise that function? That is the great paradox. I am at peace with what is. So, I close with the following prayer, which I think sums up the attitude of a true Course's dedicated student while experiencing himself as a body in a world:

> *"Lord, make me an instrument of your peace:*
> *where there is hatred, let me sow love;*
> *where there is injury, pardon;*
> *where there is doubt, faith;*
> *where there is despair, hope;*
> *where there is darkness, light;*
> *where there is sadness, joy.*

O divine Master, grant that I may not so much seek to be consoled as
to console,
to be understood as to understand,
to be loved as to love.

For it is in giving that we receive,
it is in pardoning that we are pardoned,
and it is in dying that we are born to eternal life.
Amen."

-San Francisco de Asís

Made in the USA
Monee, IL
10 August 2024